Michael Asher
Kunsthalle Bern, 1992

Anne Rorimer

One Work Series Editor
Mark Lewis

Afterall Books Editorial Directors
Charles Esche and Mark Lewis

Editor
Pablo Lafuente

Managing Editor
Gaia Alessi

Associate Editor
Caroline Woodley

Editorial Assistant
Francesca Colussi and Louise O'Hare

Copy Editor
Deirdre O'Dwyer

One Work is a unique series of books published by Afterall, based at Central Saint Martins College of Art and Design in London. Each book presents a single work of art considered in detail by a single author. The focus of the series is on contemporary art and its aim is to provoke debate about significant moments in art's recent development.

Over the course of more than one hundred books, important works will be presented in a meticulous and generous manner by writers who believe passionately in the originality and significance of the works about which they have chosen to write. Each book contains a comprehensive and detailed formal description of the work, followed by a critical mapping of the aesthetic and cultural context in which it was made and has gone on to shape. The changing presentation and reception of the work throughout its existence is also discussed, and each writer stakes a claim on the influence 'their' work has on the making and understanding of other works of art.

The books insist that a single contemporary work of art (in all of its different manifestations), through a unique and radical aesthetic articulation or invention, can affect our understanding of art in general. More than that, these books suggest that a single work of art can literally transform, however modestly, the way we look at and understand the world. In this sense the *One Work* series, while by no means exhaustive, will eventually become a veritable library of works of art that have made a difference.

First published in 2012
by Afterall Books

Afterall
Central Saint Martins
College of Art and Design,
University of the Arts London
Granary Building
1 Granary Square
London N1C 4AA
www.afterall.org

ISBN Paperback: 978–1–84638–093–8
ISBN Cloth: 978–1–84638–092–1

Distribution by The MIT Press,
Cambridge, Massachusetts and London
www.mitpress.mit.edu

Art Direction and Typeface Design
A2/SW/HK

Printed and bound by
Die Keure, Belgium

The *One Work* series is printed
on FSC-certified papers

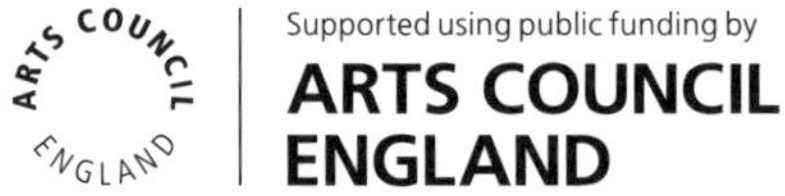

Michael Asher
Kunsthalle Bern, 1992

Anne Rorimer

This book could not have been written without the long-term
support and friendship of Michael Asher. Since 1980, when
I first determined to articulate some aspects pertaining to his
groundbreaking career, Asher has given extensively of his time.
I have greatly benefited from many conversations with him over
the years – conversations that have sharpened my understanding
of his multifaceted production, although they also have lead
to the humbling realisation that in these pages I have only dealt
with the tip of the iceberg. I am also indebted to the professional
editorial insights of Betsy Zinn Stepina, who read the initial
draft of my manuscript in advance of submission. I further
wish to thank Yoko Kanayama, Michael Asher's assistant,
for her tremendous help and always prompt replies to my
questions and the requests initiated by the Afterall editors.
The editors would also like to thank Michael Asher and Yoko
Kanayama for their help and generosity during the preparation
and production of this book as well as Elfriede Schalit and
Karin Minger at Kunsthalle Bern for their support in providing
information from archive.

Anne Rorimer is a freelance curator and art historian specialising
in art after 1965. She began her career at the Art Institute of
Chicago, where she exhibited the work of Michael Asher in
the late 1970s and early 1980s. She was the co-curator, with
Ann Goldstein, of 'Reconsidering the Object of Art: 1965–
1975', held at the Museum of Contemporary Art, Los Angeles
in 1995–96. In addition to articles for periodicals including
Artforum and *October*, she has contributed essays on many
occasions to exhibition catalogues. She is the author of *New
Art in the 60s And 70s: Redefining Reality* (Thames & Hudson,
London, 2001/2004).

For A, B, C and J

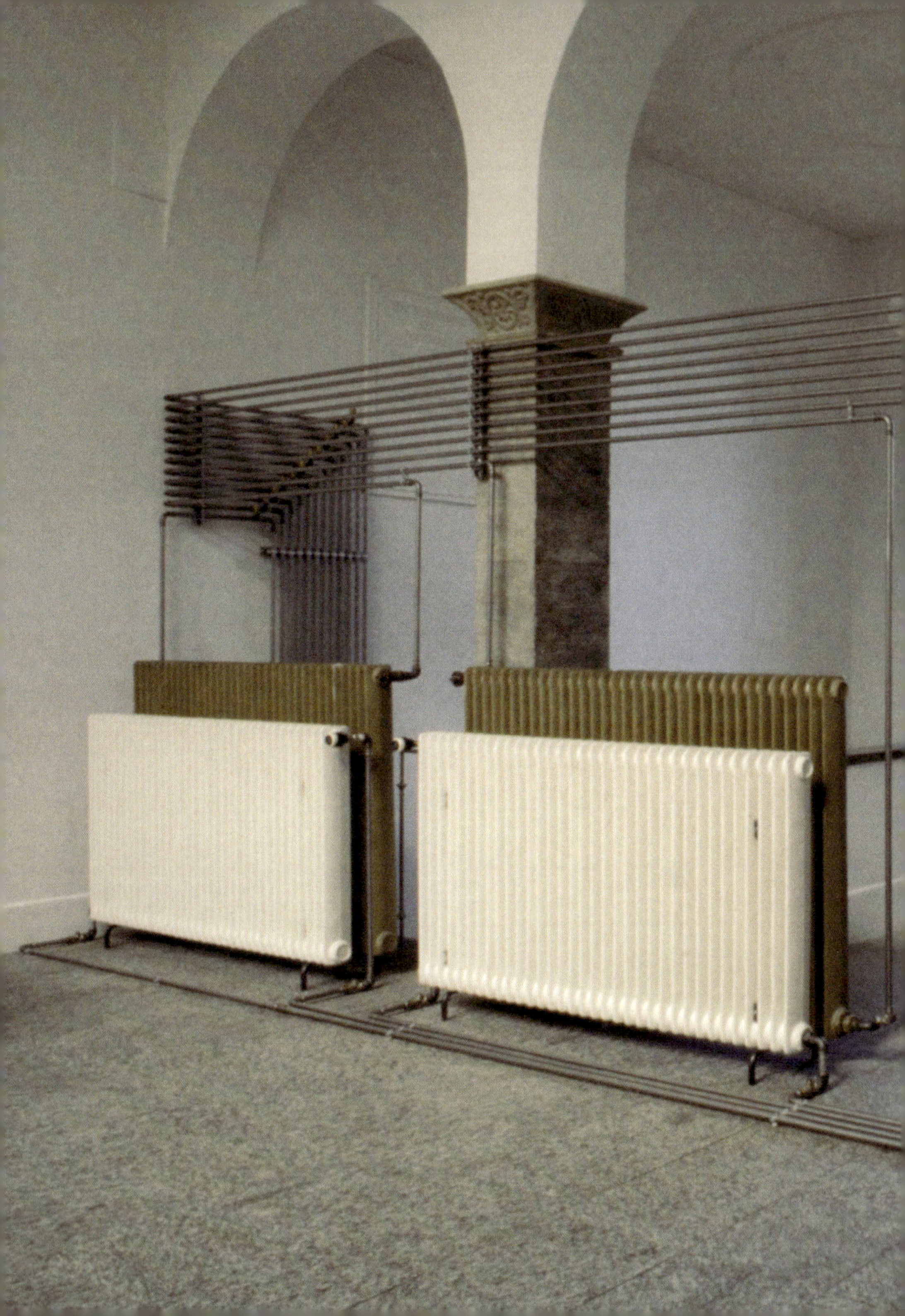

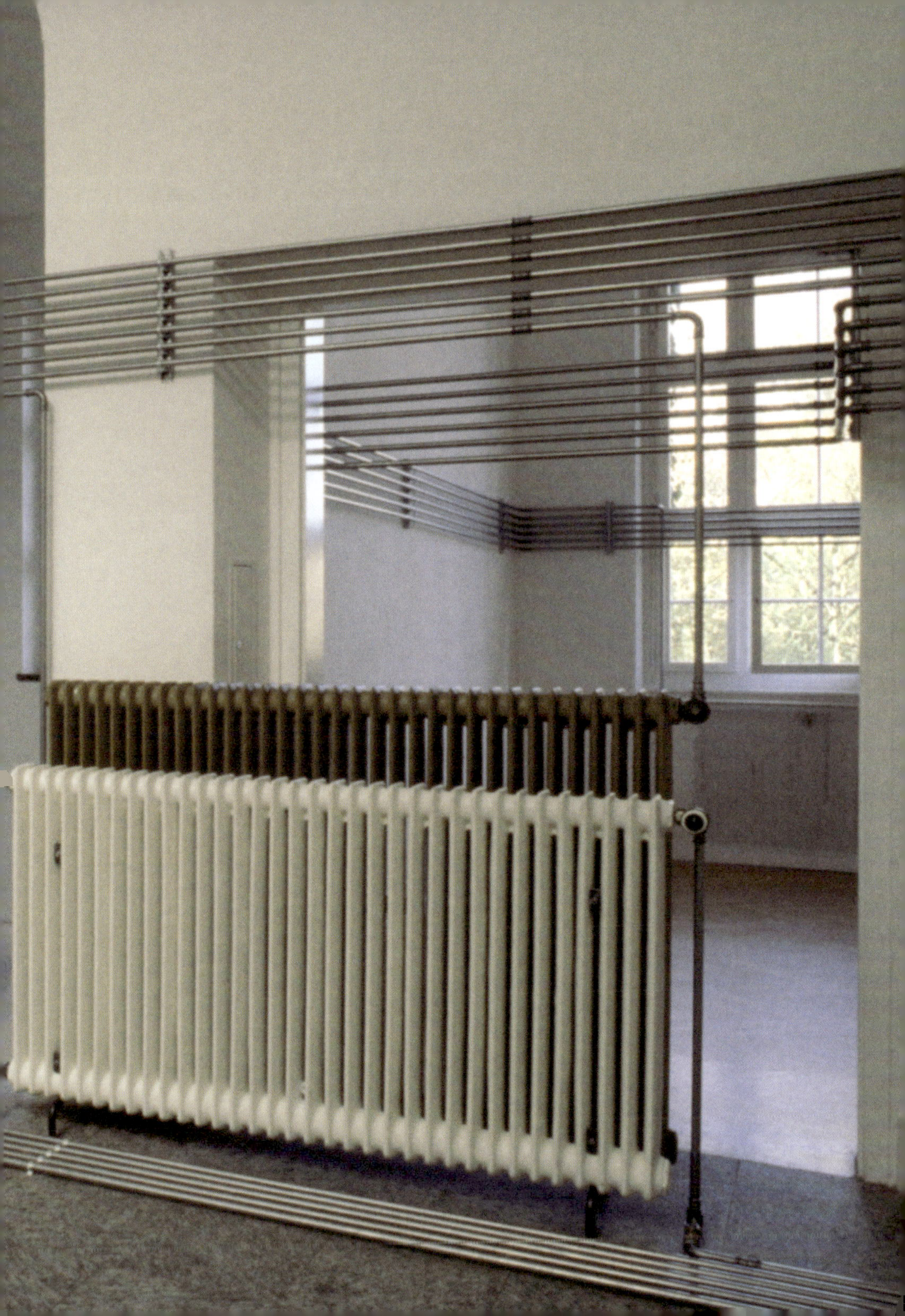

cover and previous pages

Michael Asher,
Kunsthalle Bern, Bern, Switzerland,
October 16—November 29, 1992,
1992

Contents

Michael Asher's Work for Bern

Upon entry into the Kunsthalle Bern during Michael Asher's solo exhibition, *Kunsthalle Bern, Bern, Switzerland, October 16 — November 29, 1992* (1992; fig.1—16), which took place from 16 October to 29 November 1992, visitors were presented with a striking display. In lieu of individually placing objects in one or more of the Kunsthalle's seven galleries and two floors, Asher installed nineteen radiators in its first room. With the exception of two units on either side of the main doorway of the entryway gallery, which were immovable fixtures permanently encased in lidded stone containers resembling ancient Roman sarcophagi,[1] Asher garnered the other seventeen radiators from their usual locations throughout the public areas of the institution (fig.1). The two units provided the key to the formation of the work, since they were already — and inextricably — in place.

Asher situated the radiators in the entrance gallery in accordance with their original positions and orientations in the rooms from which they were removed. The rectangular heating units were a variety of heights and widths. Some were placed parallel to walls or nearby radiators; others related perpendicularly to the surrounding walls or units. Four tall free-standing radiators of equal height, angled at each of the four corners and facing inward, formed a separately defined enclave within the overall gallery enclosure. These units had roughly painted backs, as opposed to pristinely maintained fronts, signalling their former placement in niches (fig.2). The variously painted, shaped and scaled radiators either hugged the walls or stood out from them. Thus amassed, the units compactly filled the gallery, blocking one of three doorways. Nonetheless, visitors had adequate leeway to walk past the radiators to begin following the routes taken by steel pipes connecting the relocated units to their original valves,[2] that led from the radiators to other parts of the museum, denuded of paintings and sculpture.[3]

These tubular conduits — coursing in linear fashion along the Kunsthalle's walls — made possible the continued use of the radiators by allowing for the transport of hot water from the boilers located in the basement. The displacement affected the temperature of the Kunsthalle unevenly. The exhibition took place during a cold winter (Asher recalls there were snowstorms the day after the opening),[4] and the accumulation of heating units in one room created a differential of temperature between it and the other rooms.[5]

Whereas the radiators served as the work's primary material form, the tubular pipes — visually and functionally connecting each unit to the heat source — imbued the installation with compelling and directional lines of force. With the aid of a consulting architect, Asher determined the most efficient route for the hot-water pipes to travel from valves to radiators. Installed so that the first was placed just below the lintel of the doors, the pipes ran singly or in multiples that, in some places, converged in parallel rows of as many as a dozen tubular elements. They ran along every wall and, per force, through all the doorways between galleries. By means of fitted elbow joints at architectural junctures, the pipes turned corners and responded to structural variances. They also paralleled the slant of the staircase leading to the lower-level galleries (fig.15 and 16), and spanned the empty space between the columns supporting the arches that surround the stairwell beneath the Kunsthalle's leaded-glass skylight (fig.1, 5 and 13).

The transformation of the Kunsthalle Bern in *Kunsthalle Bern, Bern, Switzerland, October 16—November 29, 1992*[6] was a monumental aesthetic achievement. It evidences not only an apparent rejection of the traditional material nature of sculpture, but also Asher's deft ability to find unconventional methods by which to represent, in ever-shifting perceptible

terms, the invisible systems underlying the collection, housing
and display of art in museums and galleries. It is evidence of
Asher's major role in spearheading the creation of works imbued
with a self-conscious awareness of their dependence on their
exhibition contexts.

Ulrich Loock, the exhibition's organiser and director of the
Kunsthalle Bern in 1992, concluded his introductory catalogue
essay by underscoring the work's dual nature:

> *With this kind of work by Michael Asher the working of
> the institution of art is subjected to critical analysis and
> it is stressed that the postulated autonomy of the artwork
> is really dependent on the effectiveness of the museum
> apparatus. But at the same time this work, the exhibited
> heating system, also presents an exemplary alternative,
> being readable as a paradigm for a still-functional,
> utilitarian work within the field of art.*[7]

Loock's fellow catalogue authors, Birgit Pelzer and Dieter
Schwarz, also observed the paradigmatic dimension of a work
based on a displacement of givens rather than on an installation
of objects brought in from outside institutional confines and
subsequently returned to collectors or subjected to processes
of purchase and sale at the end of the exhibition. Commenting
that Asher represents the space that an object has occupied
rather than the object itself,[8] Pelzer later noted the important
fact — or bottom line, one might ironically say — that the
Bern work could not be 'reduced to the terms of exchange, nor
to the relationship of exchange'.[9] Principally, Pelzer focused
on how the work relied on circulation and the creation of paths
of energy that ended up, economically speaking, devoid of market
value. Schwarz also took the functional aspect of the radiators
into consideration, and, furthermore, emphasised the work as

a critique of the discreteness of serially based Minimal
sculpture:

> *If Minimalist sculptures are discrete objects negating
> any contextual relationship to the space surrounding them
> other than its strict function as the container making their
> perception possible, then Asher introduces a subtle reversal
> in his use of radiators. On the one hand the heating units
> are [...] defined objects with distinct formal qualities, in the
> same way as [are] the sequences of pipes which primarily
> determine the galleries. On the other hand, as they
> continue in operation, and perceptibly so by producing heat,
> discharging so to speak an excess of meaning — in this way
> they present a grotesque and distorted model of Minimalist
> sculpture.*[10]

An engineering and intellectual feat, the Bern work radically
diverged from the Minimal practice to which it referred
(although the formal precision of the installation recalled
some aspects of Minimalism). By relocating the radiators to
the entryway gallery and connecting them back to the point
of their original installation, Asher integrated his exhibition
with the entire institution, bringing its galleries together as
a single unit.[11]

Connections to Context, 1990–92

Directly preceding the Bern work, at the outset of the 1990s, Asher executed five solo exhibitions — exhibitions that demonstrate both the enormously diverse nature of his methodology and the connection of the material body of each work to realities relating to its site. Additionally, and most significantly, Asher grounded these exhibitions in their institutional context through pertinent socio-economic, political, geographical and historical information. As with *Kunsthalle Bern, 1992*, and using disparate means in each presentation — but often addressing issues of flow and circulation — he furthered his ongoing exploration of methods by which to invest the art object with a built-in contextual frame of reference rather than with monetary value. The five exhibitions — which took place in Chicago, at the Renaissance Society (1990); in Villeurbanne, at the Nouveau Musée (1991); in Dijon, at Le Consortium (1991); in Paris, at the Centre Pompidou (1991); and in Brussels, at the Palais des Beaux-Arts (1992) — evince the multifarious nature of Asher's modus operandi in his quest to bring into view otherwise invisible factors relevant to the exhibition space.

The Renaissance Society at the University of Chicago, Chicago, Illinois, U.S.A., January 21—March 4, 1990 (1990; fig.27—30) consisted of three free-standing maroon wall partitions displaying panels with text and photographs. He allied the information printed on the panels with the exhibition space by identifying three types of factory-made hardware around the perimeter of the gallery, which he demarcated with 10-centimetre high maroon numerals to match the colour of the wall on which the text panels were mounted.[12] Number '1' corresponded with a window chain (fig.29), number '2' with the radiator enclosure running along the baseline of the room and number '3' with a sash lock on a window (fig.30). The numeric designations, almost like footnotes to a text, correlated with three US patent numbers

— 'U.S. Patent #756,481', 'U.S. Patent #2,487,287' and 'U.S. Patent #4,050,724' — that Asher stencilled on the reverse sides of the three wall partitions that bore the text panels (fig.28).

The written content of the text panels resulted from Asher's research on and excerpting of the writings of nine social scientists and educational theorists who taught at the University of Chicago between 1897 and 1909. Black-and-white photographs of the professors — among them, well-known figures such as John Dewey and Thorstein Veblen — appeared in the upper-left corners of the text panels (fig.27). The quoted material addressed the ideology underlying the American Arts and Crafts movement, which rejected the ornate in favour of rustic simplicity and the use of natural materials. As selected by Asher, the writings of the nine professors coincided with the heyday of the movement's activities around the turn of the twentieth century, and its influence on the country's progressive educational system as well as on individual designers and architects such as, most notably, Gustav Stickley and Frank Lloyd Wright. The movement's thesis revolved around the belief that the creation of handmade objects for decorative use would provide an antidote to the exigencies of the factory by allowing for self-expression on the part of the labourer while fostering well-designed products.[13]

With the exception of Veblen, the other eight professors promulgated the therapeutic role that education in art and in crafts could play in counteracting the ills of industrial society.[14] Asher included quotations from John Graham Brooks, a lecturer in political economics who ingenuously and perhaps simplistically argued for the production of 'better and more honest products'. Similarly, John Dewey, whose approach to education is still considered a referent today, advocated the incorporation of art into the educational system as an antidote to 'the most undesirable features of the present industrial regime'. Veblen, however, made no effort to conceal the contradictory aspects of his writing, and indeed articulated the ineffectualness of the Arts and Crafts movement as a social remedy for the machine age. In the Renaissance Society excerpts, he clearly suggests that the idealism of the Arts and Crafts movement was escapist; however, he did not propose any alternative to the complexities of industrialism.

As a supplement to his installation, Asher produced a ten-page bibliographical handout. It allowed viewers to further pursue the issues raised in the text panels, and mediated between the theoretical stances contained within them and the practical reality of the fixtures identified by the patent numbers.[15] By aggrandising unnoticed yet necessary functional parts of the exhibition space (the window chain, the radiator enclosure and the window lock), the work gave credence to the mass-produced, non-art object based on inventive creativity and principles of design. Furthermore, Asher's Renaissance Society exhibition took into account the space's affiliation with the University of Chicago (its location on campus is housed in the same building as classrooms). By linking the gallery to theories developed by once-resident and reigning minds as well as to operational hardware, the work fused with its specific site while further prying loose the ingrained belief in hands-on craftsmanship and technical skill as a requisite for ensuring not only the financial value of art, but art itself as a cultural product.

The institutional site was also the focus of Asher's three exhibitions in France during 1991, which he examined in order to re-evaluate the singular, marketable art object. Each work also explored points of intersection between the individual venue and the otherwise unobserved, or at least not explicit, contextual conditions surrounding and underlying it. To achieve this, Asher continued to utilise pre-existing elements found within each space.

For *Le Nouveau Musée, Villeurbanne, France, Opened May 22, 1991* (1991), Asher transformed once-functional equipment into a work that critiqued traditional methods of bronze casting, a process often used to give form to singular stationary objects, civic monuments or statues of heroic figures.[16] Asher took the opportunity of the museum's renovation plans and requested to use the cast-iron boilers of the building, which he melted and poured into 700 thin, hand-size, rectangular objects resembling paperweights. (Each piece measured 7.5 by 10 centimetres and gradually tapered in thicknesses from 1.5 to 1.1 centimetres; fig.31 and 32.) A raised relief text on one side of each cast-iron object referred to the renovation of the museum and stipulated who was eligible to receive the object: namely, anyone who had lost, or was at risk of losing, their home because of escalating land values and rising housing costs. A text, similarly in relief, on the other side of each iron weight declared: 'Se loger est un droit! N'accepter pas l'expulsion ou la discrimination.' ('Housing is a right! Do not accept eviction or discrimination.')[17] The telephone numbers of two local agencies devoted to helping people at the mercy of neighbourhood gentrification were also included.[18] The agencies, along with seven other social service organisations, were responsible for distributing the metal objects, which were not for sale. On the cover of the exhibition catalogue is a photograph of sprayed graffiti text stating 'Rénovation = Expulsion'.

By means of recycling the cast iron from the museum's old boilers, Asher subverted the usual cycles of art production and reception to bypass the speculative channels of buying and selling. Instead, he drew attention to social groups in the community who were left out in the cold by the vagaries of economic change and sociocultural gentrification.[19] The use of the boilers as subjects of transformation presents a clear precedent for *Kunsthalle Bern, 1992*, especially in its gaze into institutional infrastructure, but, unlike in Bern, the intervention at Villeurbanne eluded any sort of consolidated viewing inside of a building and overtly delved into the potential efficacy of the museum as a conduit to social amelioration. If *Kunsthalle Bern, 1992* examined relations inside the institution, *Le Nouveau Musée, 1992* looked outside, as the 700 iron weights abandoned the physically-defined, institutional boundaries found in Bern, to be dispersed throughout the town to citizens in need.

Le Consortium, Dijon, France, June 7—July 27, 1991 (1991) also engaged with integral heating systems.[20] Here Asher installed a work within the museum (as he would in Bern), yet he also extended it into the city (as he had in Villeurbanne). Whereas in the former work Asher would display actual radiators as sculptural forms, in Dijon he reproduced on the walls of Le Consortium schematic diagrammes of interior axial cuts of the heating systems belonging to sixteen of the city's important buildings, such as the town hall and the municipal theatre. The diagrams — painted in black on white at the original height that the heaters were installed in the basements of their respective locations — manifested themselves as clear-cut yet eccentric, seemingly abstract designs.

A set of sixteen colour postcards (fig.33 and 34), available for perusal or purchase, illustrated the boilers of the buildings whose heating systems were diagrammed on the museum walls. The photographs and identifying text on the cards correlated with the information on the labels that accompanied each drawing. In this way, the postcards served to ground the wall drawings in the functional reality of the oil burners, water heaters, pressure tanks, gauges and pipes of the sixteen furnaces.

Kunsthalle Bern, 1992 | 9

As a connective codicil to the work, Asher alluded on a wall text to the invisible bond between leisure travel and the tourist industry, through information taken from promotional literature published by the University of Savoy, 200 kilometres south of Dijon, for its tourist studies programme. The text mentioned the need for France, in the face of foreign competition, to maintain an upper hand in the business of tourism.

Asher followed a new line of thought for *Musée National d'Art Moderne, Centre Georges Pompidou, Paris, July 9—September 15, 1992* (1992).[21] His exhibition at the Centre Georges Pompidou consisted of material he culled from the Bibliothèque Publique d'Information, the library housed under the same roof as the museum and accessible by the same escalator as the exhibition areas of the Renzo Piano and Richard Rogers complex in the city's Beaubourg area. Asher did not gather his material from the printed pages of books; the work, instead, comprised 67 bits of paper left behind by readers who had used them as bookmarks. Asher observed these scraps lodged between the pages of 57 publications in the psychoanalysis section of the library. He chose this particular category, containing some one thousand volumes, because it had the fewest number of markers protruding from the books on the shelves.[22]

Forming a kind of room-size collage, Asher displayed the slips of paper equally spaced apart across a single row at eye level around the walls of three large galleries. He mounted each scrap behind a piece of glass the size of the marked page, positioning each fragment as it had fallen when he opened the book. The slips, sometimes blank or variously torn, included self-help advertisements (with guarantee of cure), a ticket stub from another library (appearing twice) and handwritten notes. Additionally, Asher identified the scraps with wall labels that supplied complete bibliographical information about the book from which the marker had been removed. In a fourth gallery, black-and-white photographs bound into a booklet documented how the fragments had lain on each of their pages prior to removal from their books, and recorded whatever surrounding text remained legible. Finally, Asher produced new bookmarks to hand out to visitors. These takeaways — with green lettering printed on grey paper in a reference to the green furniture and grey carpeting of the library — listed the photographed pages in conjunction with the library codes of the books.

The Paris work acted as a liaison between the exhibition space of the Centre Georges Pompidou, where one pays admission, and its public library on another floor of the building.[23] On another level, it brought museum visitors into contact with a domain of thought, information and knowledge, rendering the experience of art as, at least partly, a discursive experience. Fragments of paper and notations, mined by Asher from between pages of library books, together participated in an assemblage of previously disconnected and basically worthless ephemera. Like the radiators in Bern, these slips of paper formed a new whole within their art-exhibition context. Taken from their original places in library books, as were the Kunsthalle radiators from their locations in the exhibition areas, the slips of paper did not exhibit the three-dimensional material presence of the heaters, but echoed their subversion of the volumetric autonomy of Minimal sculpture in their equally ironic reference to the *papier collé* (but in Asher's case without its glue) made famous in the early twentieth century in France by Georges Braque and Pablo Picasso.

Opening only a month before the Bern exhibition, *Palais des Beaux-Arts, Brussels, September 18—November 18, 1992* (1992) also differed markedly from the Bern work in its exclusive use of textual and photographic components. Parallels between the

Brussels and Bern installations may nonetheless be drawn
with regard to the inseparability of both works from their
institutional parameters. An enumeration of the materials
shown in the two temporary exhibition spaces off of the
rotunda of the Palais (at its rue Royale entrance) gives a sense
of the intellectual intricacies of a work based on a range of
documentary, rather than three-dimensional, materials.

The exhibition spliced together otherwise totally unconnected
bodies of information related to Victor Horta, the architect
responsible for the Palais, and William Mulholland, the former
head of the Los Angeles Department of Water and Power, noted
for his major role in the construction of dams and aqueducts
in California in the early twentieth century. Asher based
his investigation of the two figures on a small page from the
notebook Horta kept on a trip to San Francisco and Los Angeles
in October 1918, on which he simply jotted: 'The city has
installed a water system. Chief Engineer of Water Department.
Mulholland.' Around this brief mention, Asher provided a
plethora of documentation concerning both men, constructing
a web of intersecting facts and fictions filled with correspondences and coincidences between the careers of two men working
in the same period but not personally known to each other.

In one of the two exhibition rooms, where both Horta and
Mulholland were identified by name, chronologies of their
respective careers made it possible to draw historical parallels
between them.[24] Addresses and construction dates for Horta's
projects ranged from 1890 through 1926, and, for Mulholland,
from 1896 through 1926. Two photographs, also in this room,
acknowledged the institutional sources for the body of archival
material that Asher integrated into his work. A black-and-white
photograph presented the Horta Museum on the rue Américaine
in Brussels, and a colour photograph illustrated the building for

the Department of Water and Power on Hope Street in Los Angeles. Together, the two images anchored the exhibition to the bricks-and-mortar reality where archival access to the historical past is preserved.

The second room, in which Horta's notebook page was shown, contained textual and photographic items — such as newspaper pages and films stills — related to Horta and Mulholland. Asher exhibited the front pages of eleven daily California papers from April 1918, containing news articles published on the occasion of Horta's lecture tour in the wake of World War I. The headlines included: 'Noted Belgian Here Tells of Teuton Vandalism'; 'Belgian Savant Will Lecture on War-Torn Beauty'; and 'Mr Horta, Famous Architect, and Wife, Arrives as Official Representative of Desolated Country's Government'.[25] Fascinating in and of themselves for their outmoded sensationalist language, the California dailies were shown in proximity to front-page articles from the Belgian press in March 1928 concerning the collapse of one of Mulholland's California dams. Various headlines assessed that there were between five hundred and a thousand victims. The press headlines brought the realities of war and disaster 'to life', one could say, within the historical framework of the Palais des Beaux-Arts installation.

If the press articles (accompanied by translations in French and Flemish) sounded a clear note of reality, the film stills introduced a fictional underbelly. Six colour stills from Harry Kümel's *Eline Vere* (1991) accompanied the clippings pertaining to Horta; four stills from Roman Polanski's *Chinatown* (1974) were displayed with the newspapers related to Mulholland. Respectively, in turn, Asher also included reproductions of two additional articles — a criticism of the Belgian film and a Los Angeles newspaper's review of *Chinatown* — as part of the installation. In brief, the commentaries served as cautionary

wake-up calls for keeping one's eyes open in the face of filmic
allure, a message that spoke directly to themes explored in the
movies: bourgeois self-satisfaction (*Eline Vere*) and capitalist
greed (*Chinatown*).

A multilayered work harbouring many levels of meaning and
a network of associations to be discovered by viewers moving
back and forth between the two galleries, the Brussels exhibition
engendered an 'encircling' of the factual chronologies, news
items, photographs, film stills and critical texts that, considered
as an ensemble, allowed Asher to establish previously unmade
connections between the two men.[26] This ongoing cycle is
evident, albeit in different fashions, in both the Brussels and
the Bern installations. Rather than radiators hooked up to
pipes through which hot water could circulate throughout
the Kunsthalle, at the Palais des Beaux-Arts Asher interwove
logically grounded bodies of information and intersecting points
of reference related to its location in Brussels. If visitors in Bern
had to circulate through the entirety of the museum to experience
the work in toto, in Brussels they could cut their own paths,
albeit mentally as well as spatially, to follow wherever the work
might lead them.

Despite their differing strategies, Asher's five solo exhibitions
immediately preceding *Kunsthalle Bern, 1992* were bound to
their institutional site in one way or another: the Renaissance
Society in connection with the history of progressive education
at the University of Chicago; the Nouveau Musée with those
who had lost their housing in Villeurbanne; the Consortium
with the interior workings of other public buildings in Dijon;
the Musée National d'Art Moderne with the Centre Georges
Pompidou's public library; and the Palais des Beaux-Arts with
the pre-eminent Art Nouveau architect Victor Horta. All five
works rested on the making of connections, both literal and

abstract, not only within the visible parameters of the work but also, most significantly, beyond its architectural borders. The exhibition in Bern similarly escaped the creation of a detachable, marketable object. In light of the five exhibitions realised just before it, *Kunsthalle Bern, 1992* extricated itself from the fate of disconnection from its original context by proposing itself simultaneously as a physical model of and a paradigmatic metaphor for connection.

With(in) and Without Museum and Gallery Walls, 1974–89

Kunsthalle Bern, Bern, Switzerland, October 16—November 29, 1992
speaks eloquently for an oeuvre devoted to recasting sculptural
practice and to redefining the discrete art object that is normally
separated from the existing reality in which it is rooted.
Realised at the midpoint of his more than four-decade career,
Asher's exhibition at the Kunsthalle Bern dramatically under-
lines how the artist upended previous aesthetic practice while
turning it inside out. The Bern work marks a culminating
moment in Asher's critique of the traditional artwork that
independently occupies indoor or outdoor physical space. By
wresting the radiators and pipes of a building's existing heating
system as material for constructing a newly-conceived sculptural
and contextual experience within and throughout its exhibition
spaces, Asher was able to fabricate a work from the Kunsthalle's
physical infrastructure. The steel pipes reconnected the
radiators in the entrance gallery to their position of origin
and continued to maintain visitor comfort, conveying heat to
varying and lesser degrees (quite literally) throughout all of the
exhibition areas. At the same time, divergences in temperature
(whether warmer than usual in the room containing the radiators or slightly chillier in the galleries on the second floor)
heightened viewers' powers of apperception on a somatic as well
as a visual level. With ironic reference to the museum refrain of
'do not touch', Asher allowed visitors to be 'touched' — without
sentiment — as sentient beings that depend on mental processing
to fully 'take hold' of a work. In short, *Kunsthalle Bern, 1992*
skilfully exempted itself from ingrained notions about visceral
or emotive 'feelings' in art by defining 'feeling' in purely
somatosensory terms.

Precedents and Early Work

Asher's eschewal of works that are 'detached', literally and
metaphorically, from architectural structures and, by extension,

from the socio-economic systems of support underlying museum
or gallery display finds precedent in the innovations by artists
working during the 1950s and 60s under the rubrics of Pop and
Minimal art. Pop and Minimal painting and sculpture offer a
backdrop for understanding Asher's dramatic shift away from
making 'free'-standing, discrete and portable objects. As an art
student at the University of California, Irvine, in the first half
of the 1960s, Asher was fully cognisant of the work of Jasper
Johns, Frank Stella and Andy Warhol, among others, who, in the
wake of Abstract Expressionism, were carrying the modernist
idea of painting as a self-referential, planar reality in previously
uncharted directions. However different their methods, Johns,
Stella and Warhol helped establish the idea that painting is
a reality unto itself by discovering ways to erase traditional
signs of authorial presence and subjectivity in their work.
Principally, they suppressed gestural brushwork, invented shapes
and images and hierarchical compositions in order to instate
the notion of painting's ideational self-sufficiency. Asher was
also familiar with the work of artists such as Donald Judd, Carl
Andre, Sol LeWitt and Robert Morris, whose respective revisions
of three-dimensional form had already broken new ground by the
mid-1960s. For their part, Judd, Andre, LeWitt and Morris made
sculptures from industrial materials that preclude modelling,
carving or other hand-worked techniques so as to reduce signs
of intercession by the artist that would disrupt the effect of
pure self-referentiality. These works paved the way for Asher
and his generation by virtue of the interplay they foster between
material form and actual space.

Works by Asher from 1966, the year he received his undergraduate
degree, bear witness to his appreciation of the self-referential
and anti-illusionistic properties of two- and three-dimensional
objects by his slightly older contemporaries. His early sculptures
presage his impending total break from the creation of objects

divorced from their settings. For example, he has pointed out that
his shallow, heat-moulded, transparent plexiglas works of 1966,
all untitled, of different sizes and colours, and with rounded
corners, are intended to visually 'flow into the wall'.[27]

The all-encompassing, light-filled installations of Dan Flavin
(fig.36) offer a significant precedent for Asher's evolving interest in revealing the backing systems behind the exhibition of art,
including, most basically, the walls and architectural features
of museum and gallery spaces. Flavin has mainly been associated
with the methods and principles of Minimalism, although he
anticipated the practices of installation art, which developed
in the late 1960s in tandem with works labelled under the rubric
of Conceptual art. When, in 1963, Flavin came to the idea of
substituting the light from fluorescent fixtures mounted on the
wall for pigment applied to canvas, he laid the groundwork for
artists who have contended with the entirety of the exhibition
area as a container. By mid-decade, Flavin had recognised 'that
the actual space of a room could be disrupted and played with by
careful, thorough composition of the illuminating equipment'.[28]
He had also noted his 'considered attempt to poise silent
electric light in crucial concert point to point, line by line
and otherwise in the box that is a room'.[29] Thus, as opposed to
the self-contained sculpture of Andre, Judd, LeWitt and Morris,
Flavin's room-based, literally self-reflective installations
inseparably conjoin fluorescent bulbs with light-washed
interiors to erase the dividing line between an object and its
exhibition space.

Unlike Dan Flavin's work, in which fluorescent fixtures
imported into the exhibition space remain separate, if codepen-
dent, from their supporting walls, the walls or architectural
features of an exhibition space in Asher's works, from 1969
onwards, are drawn into the material and thematic parameters

of the exhibition itself. Asher's *Writings 1973—1983 on Works 1969—1979* (1983) commences with his description of his participation in a group show at the San Francisco Art Institute, organised by Eugenia Butler and held from 11 April to 3 May 1969:

> *The work at the San Francisco Art Institute was defined exclusively by the gallery's pre-existing architectural elements and visible equipment. Givens were considered to be those elements that were not prefabricated or produced and not inserted from outside into the existing institution for the production of the work.*[30]

Asher here utilised the gallery's interlocking, modular wall panels. Instead of treating the panels in the usual manner — as dividers for altering the layout of the space or as backdrops for displaying art — he employed nine of the units as an artwork in its own right. Taped together at the seams, the panels formed an 11-metre-long partition that jutted out from a perimeter wall. The structure stretched across almost the entire length of the gallery, separating the space into two areas. Visitors entered a smaller section with relatively low lighting and were then invited to perambulate the end of the dividing wall to enter a larger, better-lit space beneath a skylight. In a move without precedent, Asher joined the museum's display panels together in order to engender a work that transformed equal-sized wall units into a sculpture, which, in turn, relied on already existing architectural reality. The complete union of sculpture and architecture extended almost unrecognisably the use of pre-existing imagery, materials or objects typified by Pop and Minimal production. Furthermore, as opposed to the nearly contemporaneous and similarly enterable *Corridor* installations (1969—72) by Bruce Nauman — with their specific agenda related to experiential, bodily interaction by viewers — it might parenthetically be observed that Asher's work circumvented the need for the introduction of secondary materials required for making Nauman's works.

A month later, for 'The Appearing/Disappearing Image/Object' exhibition at the Newport Harbor Art Museum in California (now the Orange County Museum of Art), Asher further 'attempted to avoid specific, formally ordered art-object materiality'.[31] In this work, along with a subsequent one created for the historic show 'Anti-Illusion: Procedures/Materials' at the Whitney Museum of American Art in New York, Asher employed currents of air to alter perceptual conditions. At the Whitney, a curtain of air was blown from a unit concealed above a passageway between two exhibition areas.[32] Made of the all-pervasive yet imperceptible substance required for existence, the plane of air did not visibly alter the museum architecture as would an obdurate object. Rather, it created an invisible installation detectable only on a haptic level — a harbinger of Asher's incorporation of the invisible temperature variations that would play a part much later on in Bern.

For 'Spaces', a group exhibition that opened on 30 December 1969 at the Museum of Modern Art in New York, Asher featured perceptual conditions with direct connections to the work's institutional context. In lieu of fashioning a discrete object for placement in a room, he constructed a space that could be entered. The walls of the space absorbed sound in proportion to a visitor's distance from one of its two openings — one for entry and one for exit — located diagonally opposite from each other. As visitors moved toward and away from the openings, ambient sounds progressively diminished or increased, as did the light levels closer or farther from the doorways; both sound and light were at their lowest in the centre of the room.

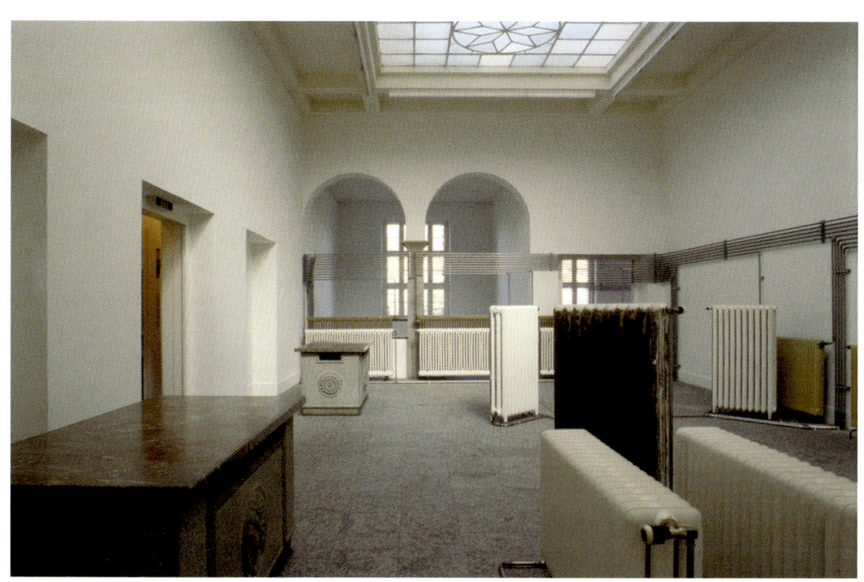

1—16. Michael Asher,
Kunsthalle Bern, Bern, Switzerland,
October 16 — November 29, 1992, 1992

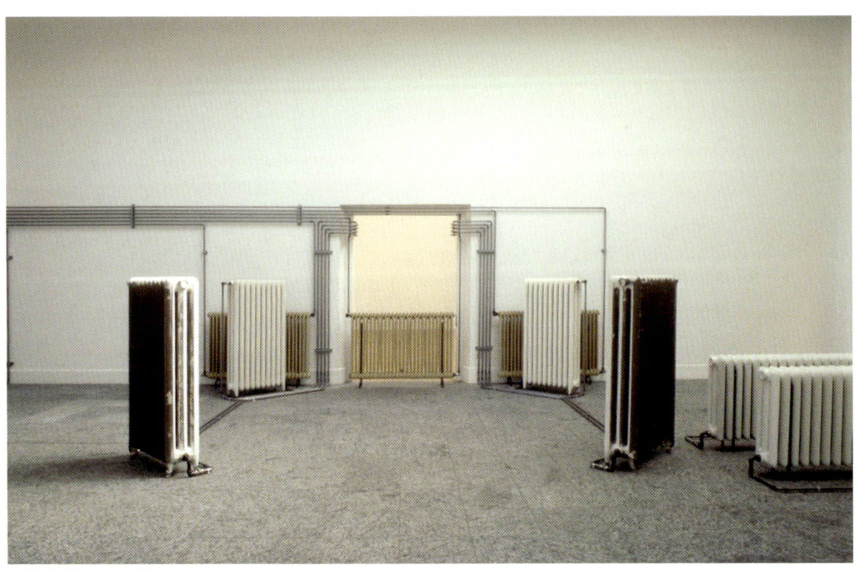

2.

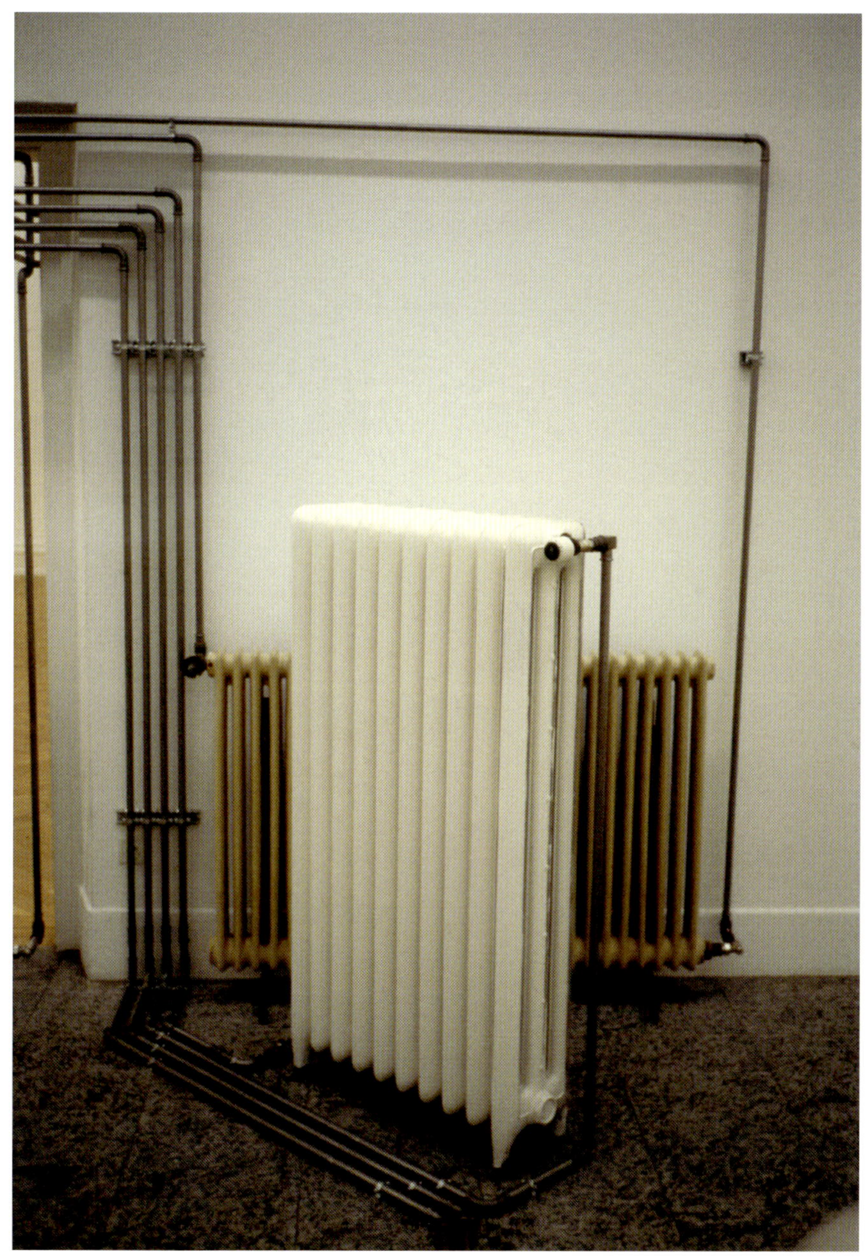

3.

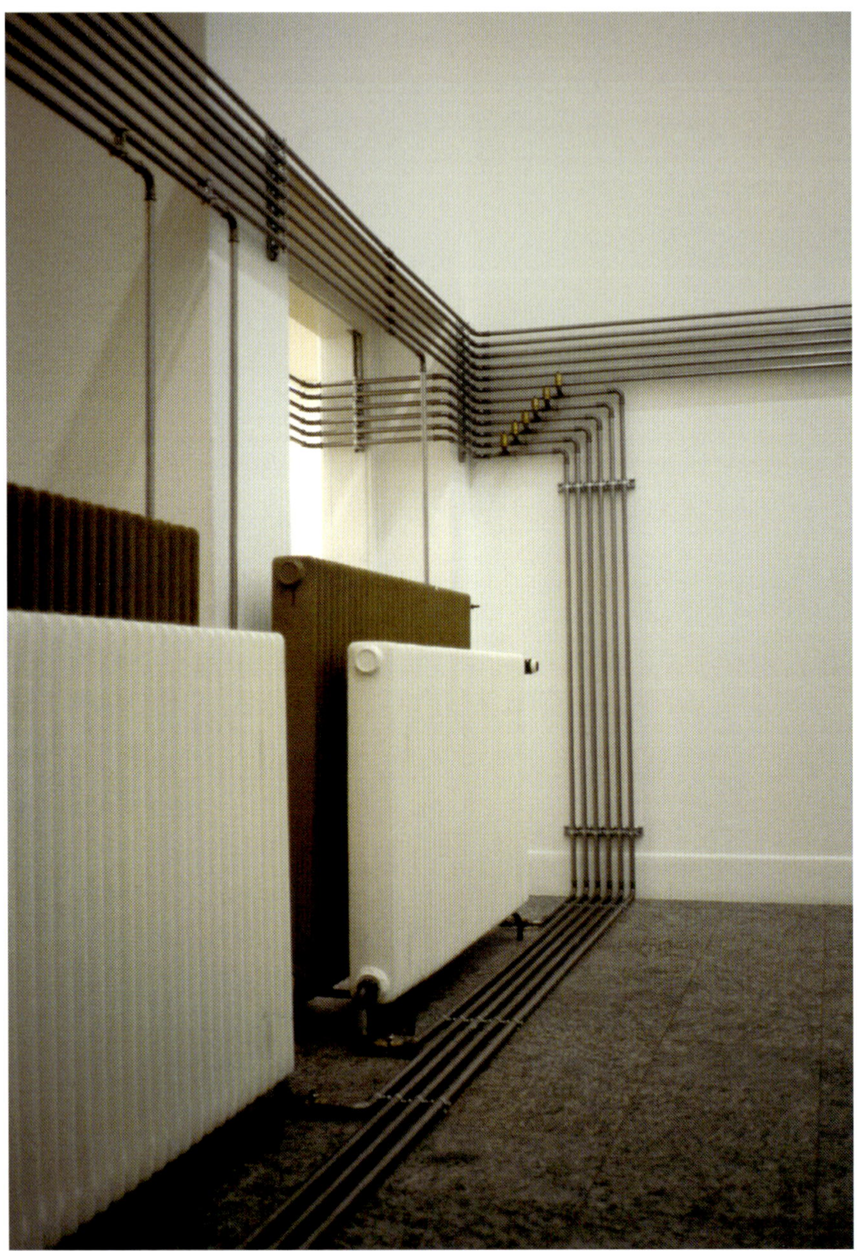

4.

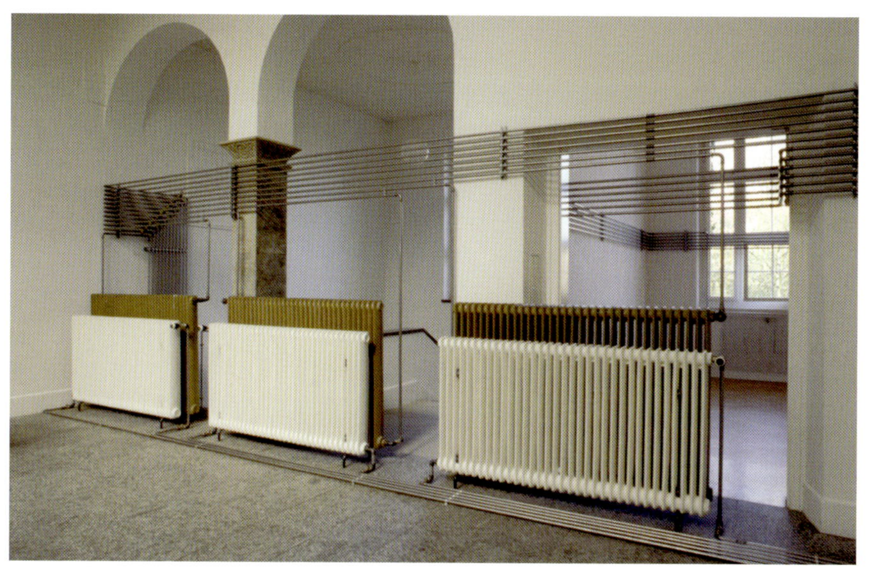

5.

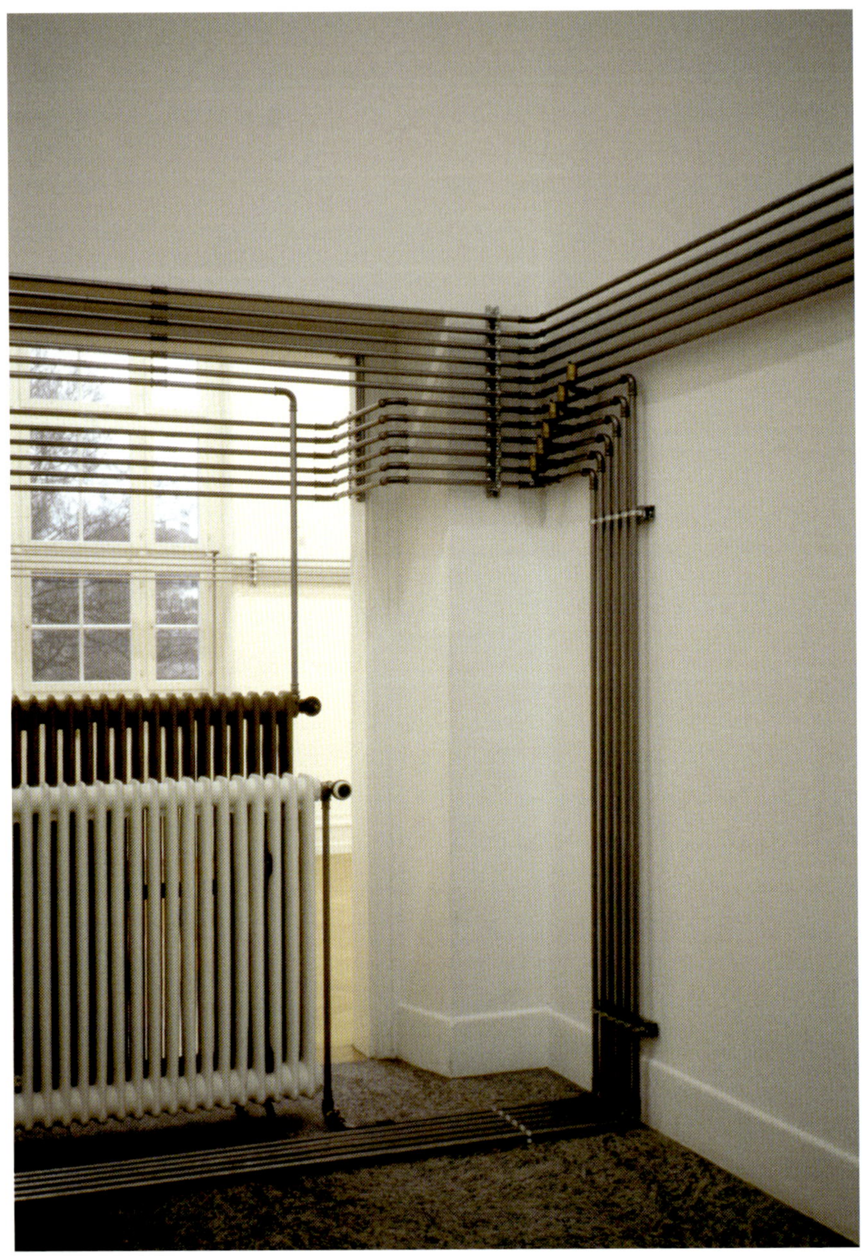

6.

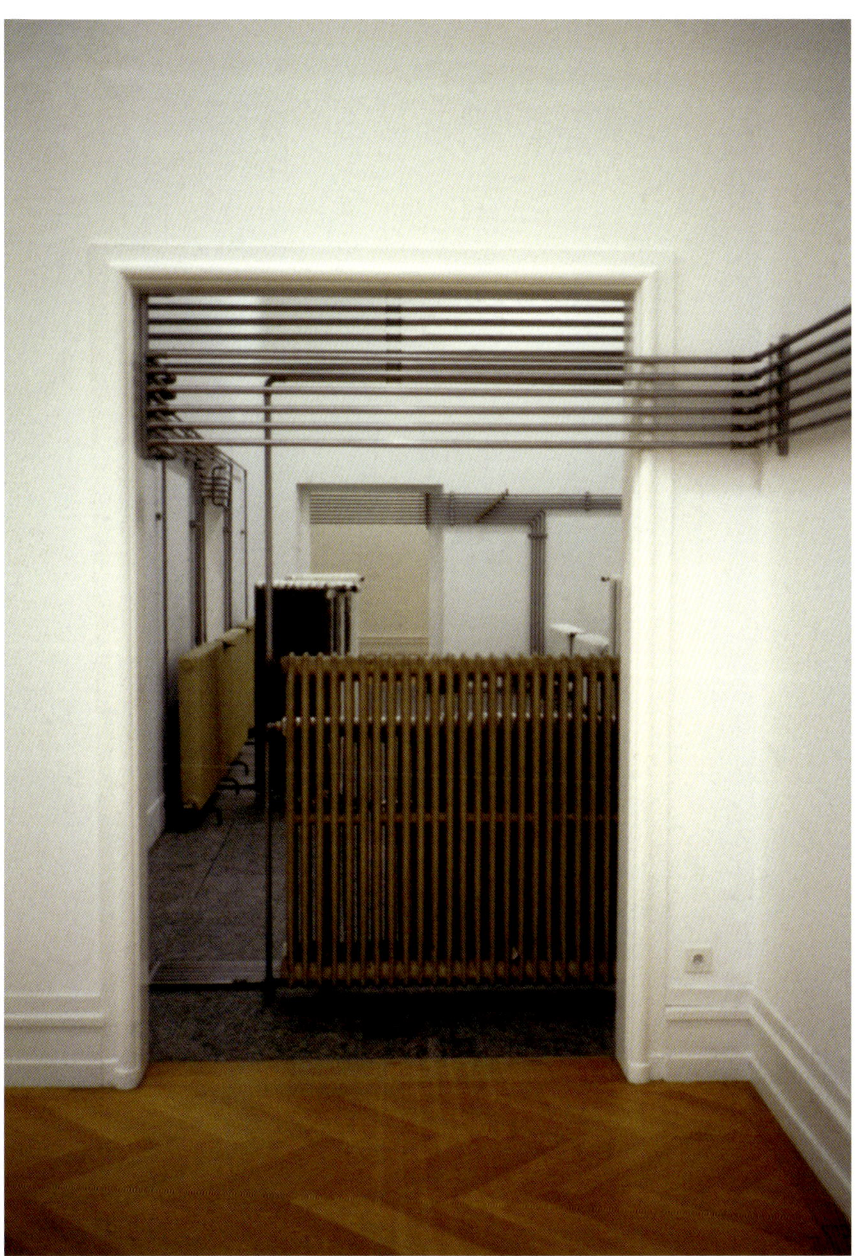

7.

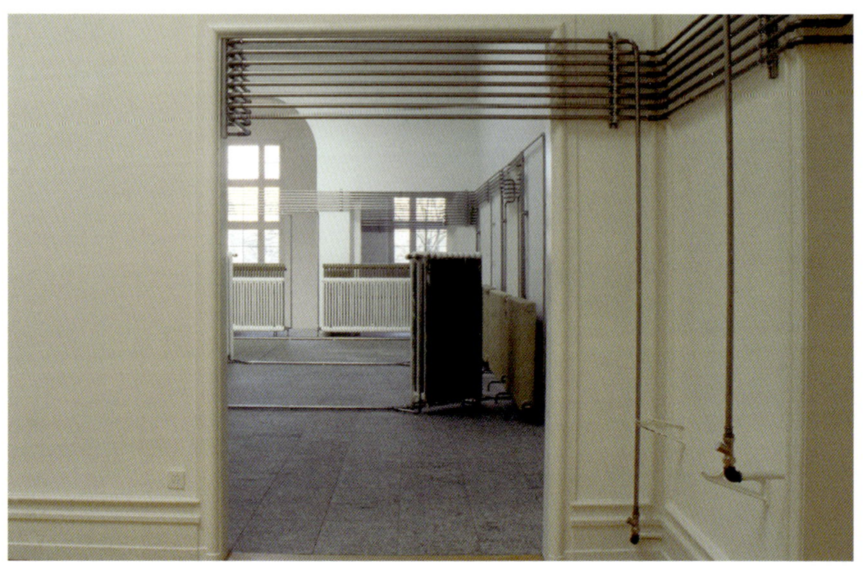

8.

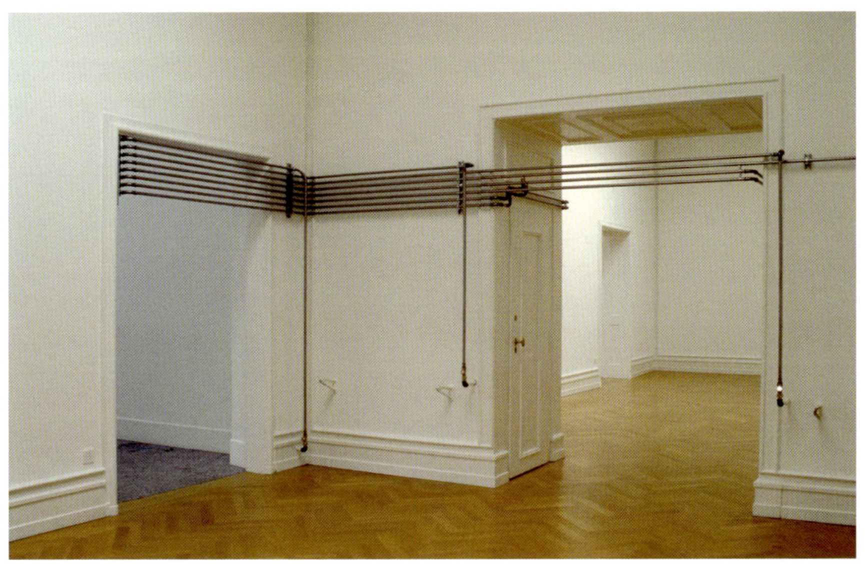

9.

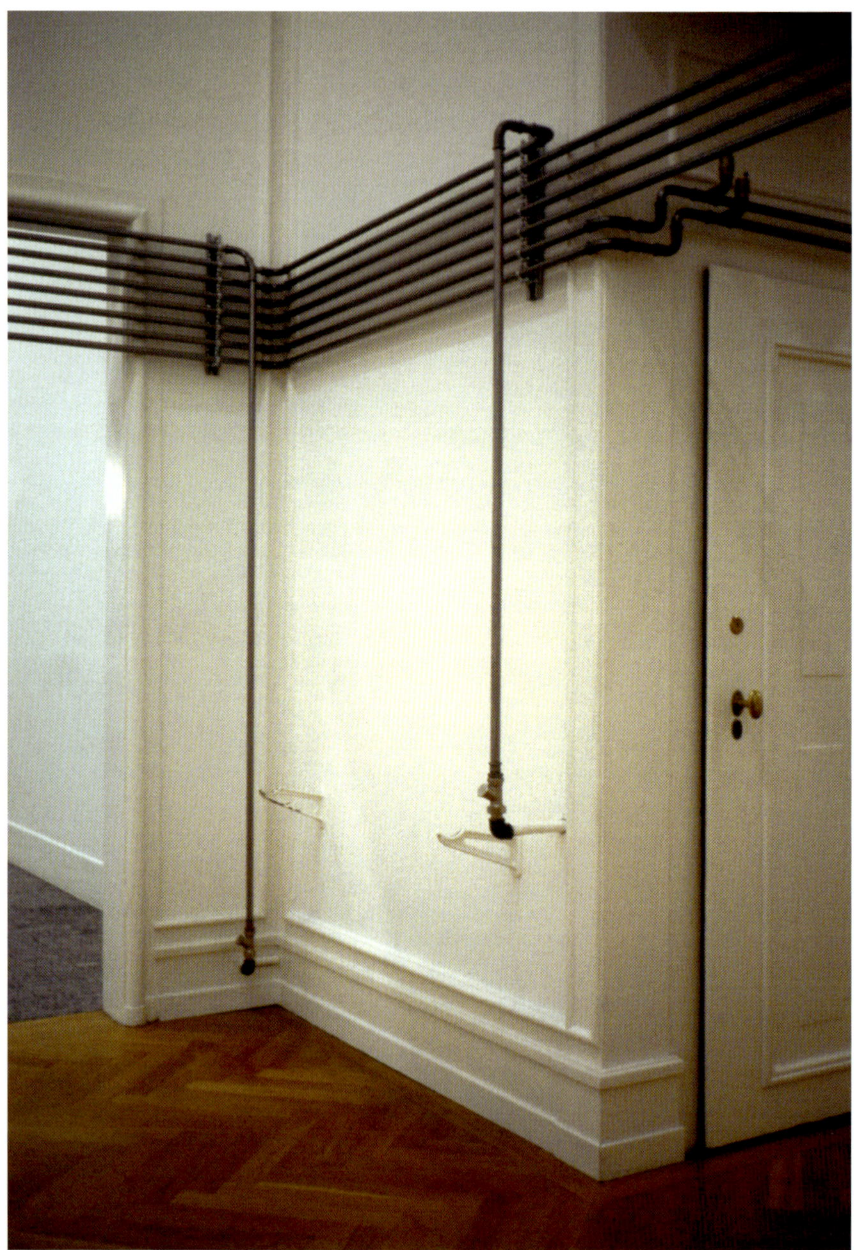

10.

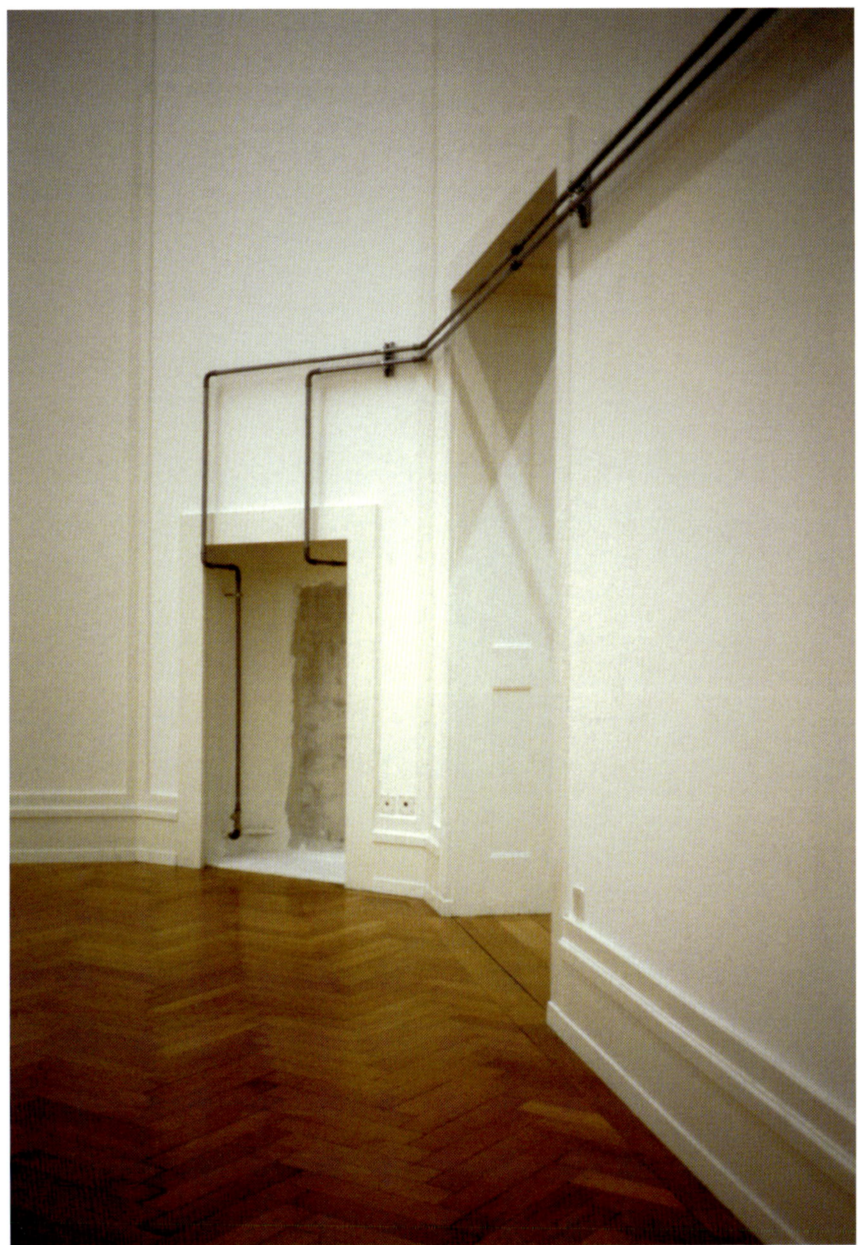

11.

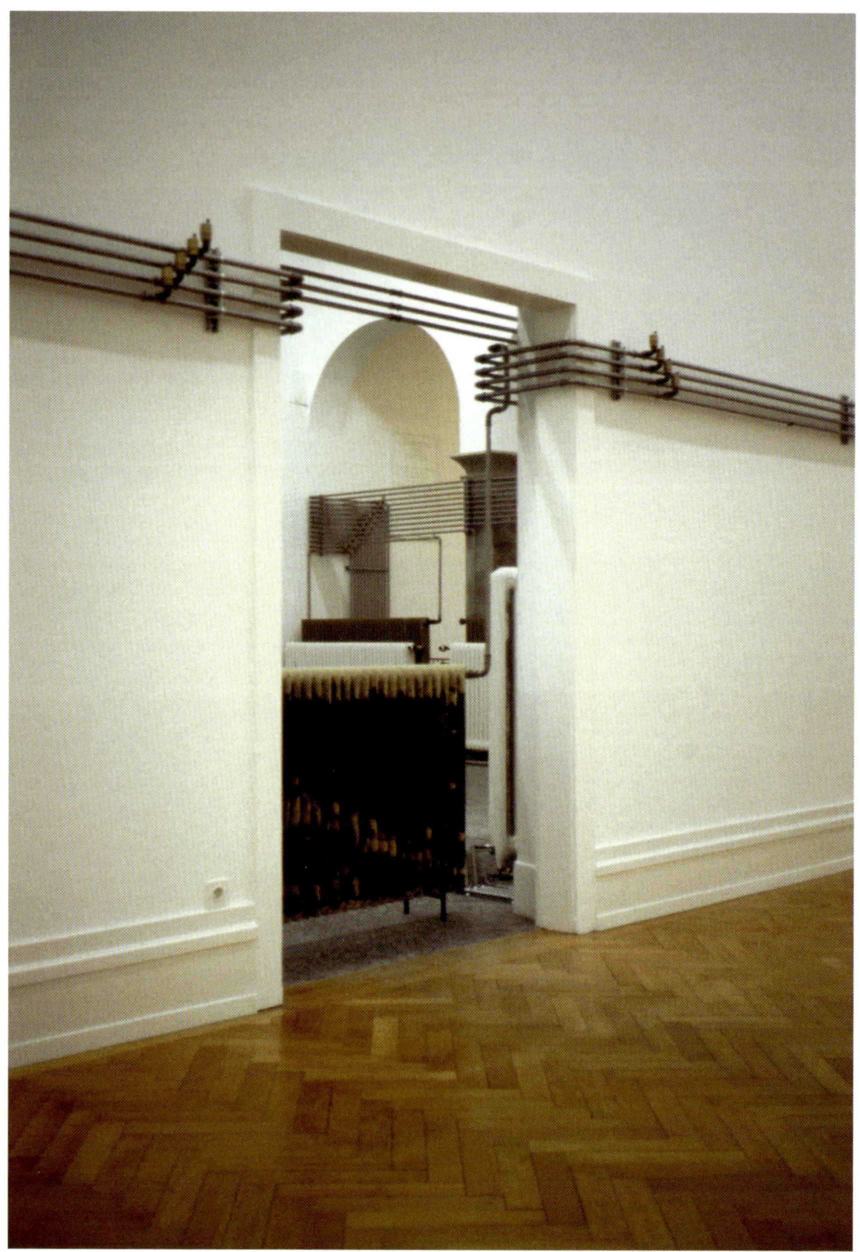

12.

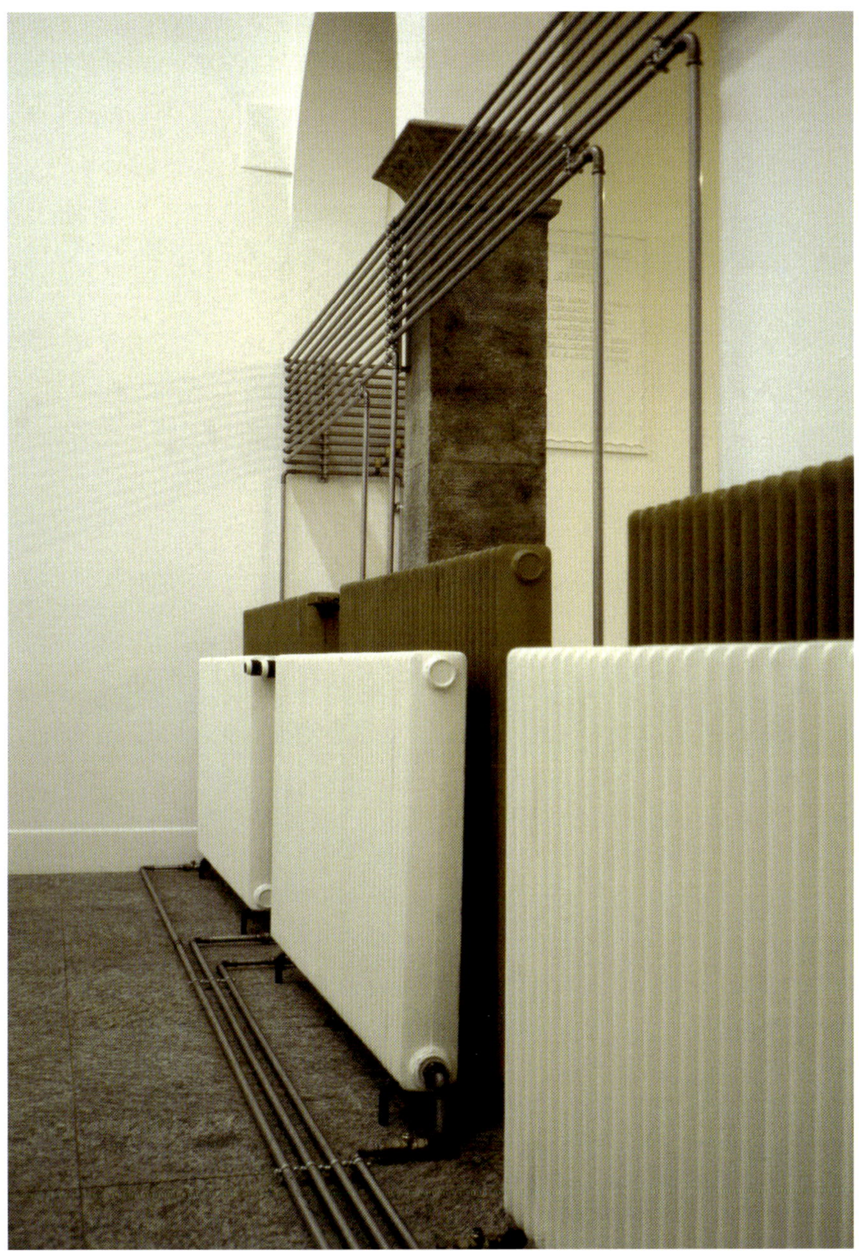

13.

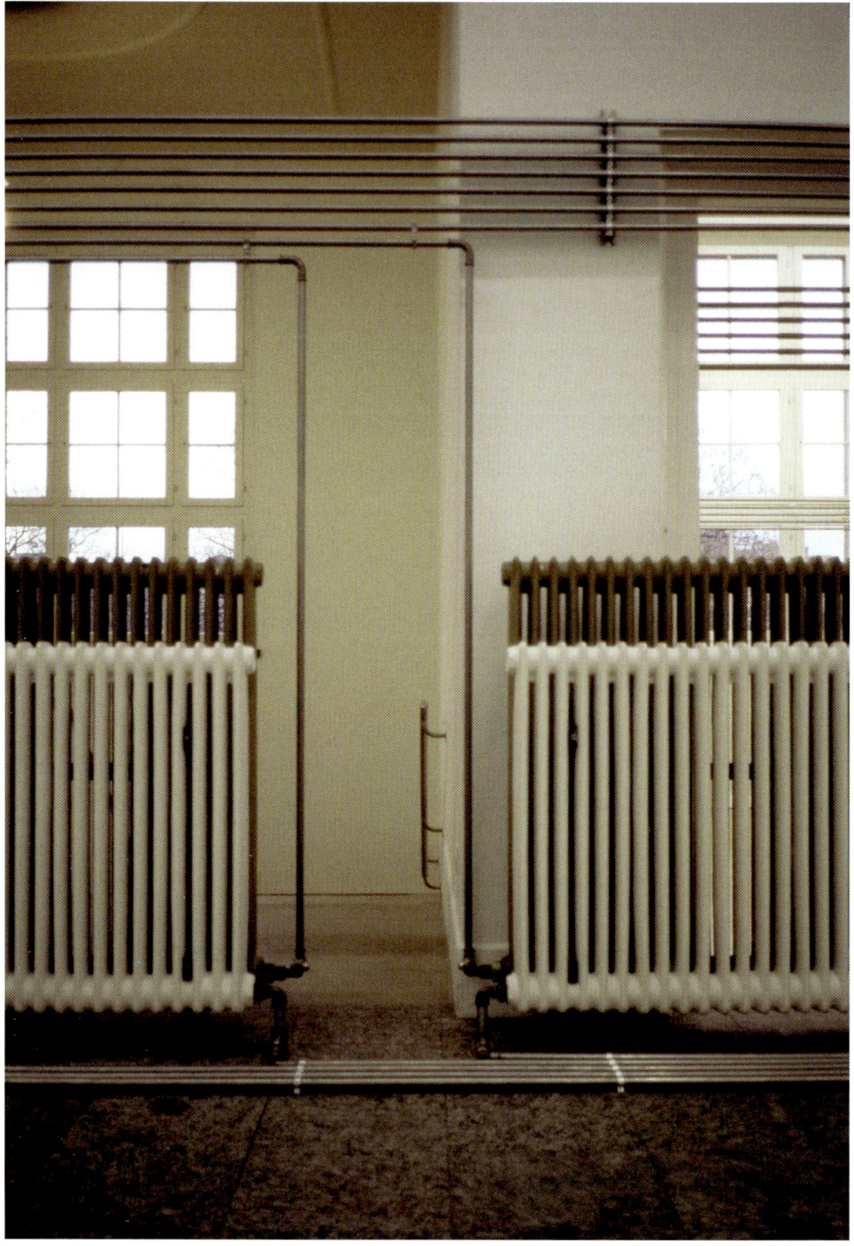

14.

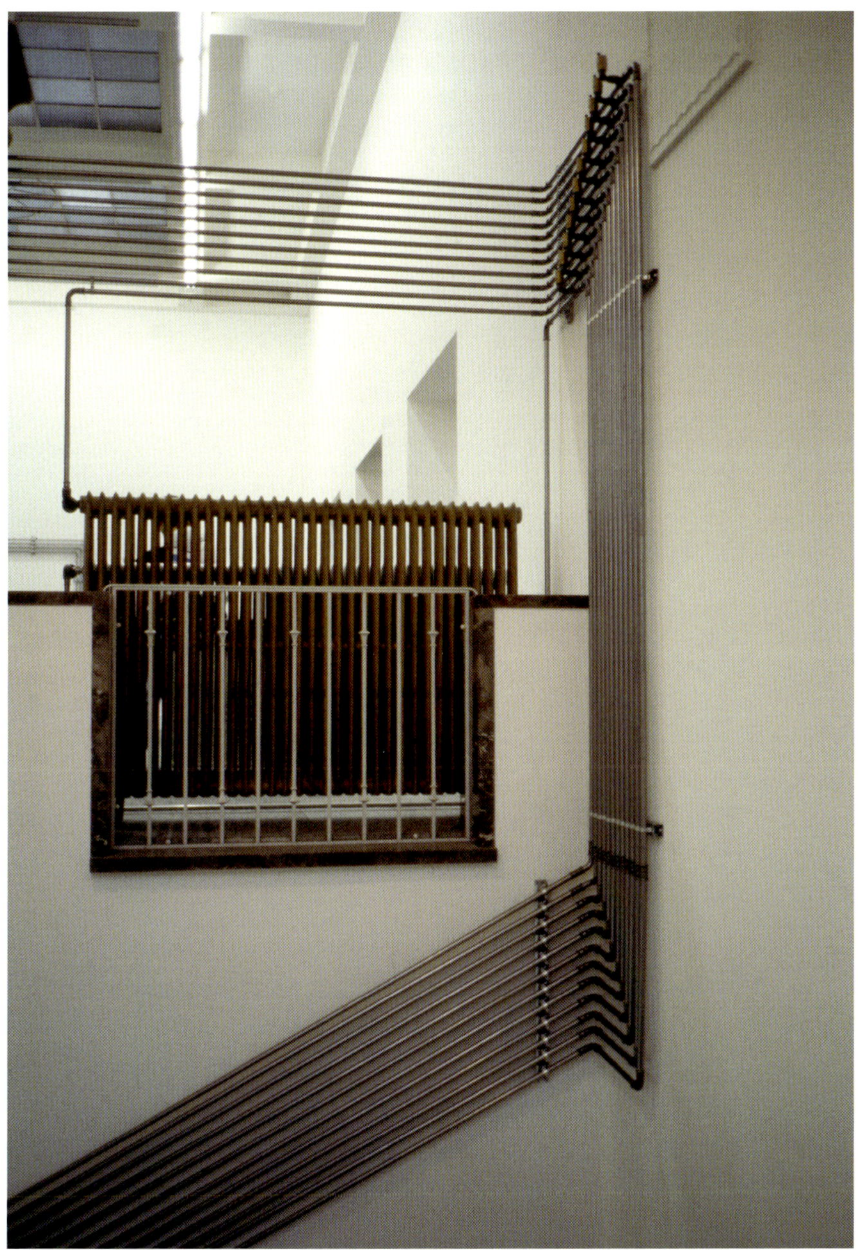

15.

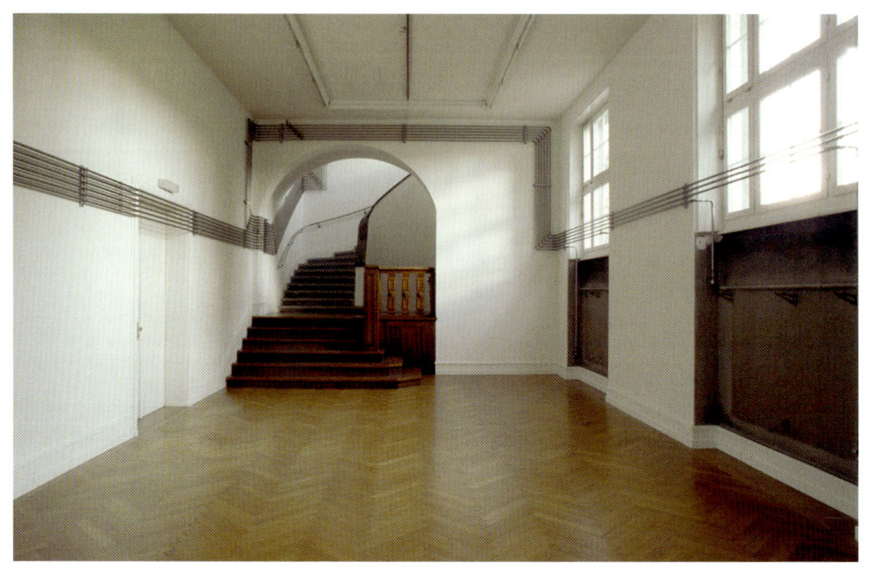

16.

By the time of his exhibition at the Galleria Toselli in Milan
in 1973, Asher had developed other means of accomplishing the
dissolution of an art object that is separated from its container.
For this show, Asher requested the removal of all paint from
the gallery's walls and ceiling. Four days of sandblasting many
layers of white paint yielded a rich brown plaster surface, which
blended with the grey concrete floor. Effectively, Asher presented
the gallery space itself as the finished work. As he explained,
'the withdrawal of the white paint, in this case, became the
objectification of the work'.[33] In anticipation of his exhibition
at the Kunsthalle Bern in 1992, the Toselli show furthered
his investigation into ways of adopting available functional
elements of a museum or gallery as essential components of
an artwork. As so clearly demonstrated in Bern, these elements
have served as the 'building blocks', one could say, of artworks
that are materially derived from and thematically grounded
in the architectural and institutional context they inhabit.

❈❈❈

Kunsthalle Bern, 1992 clearly evidences how Michael Asher
creates works that are anchored by the contextual conditions of
their display — the result of his interest in directly responding
to individual elements of the venue inviting him to exhibit.
Always adapting to the conditions of their place of exhibition,
usually — but not always (in the case of private collections or
public commissions) — at the invitation of a museum or gallery,
Asher's body of work may be categorized in three ways. First,
and earliest, are exhibitions taking place inside museums
or galleries. Second are installations that have incorporated
artworks belonging to specific museums. And third are works
that Asher realised under the aegis of an institution or organisation but away from the premises of a dedicated building.

Inside Museums and Galleries

The following discussion details the multifarious methods and
facets of Asher's probing aesthetic ingenuity in order to provide
a broad frame of reference in which to place *Kunsthalle Bern,
Bern, Switzerland, October 16—November 29, 1992*. These methods
have allowed him not only to bypass the creation of commercially
viable objects exposed to the whims of the financial system, but
they have also led to works that pointedly evidence the economic
activity at the bedrock of institutional practices revolving
around collecting and exhibiting art. His production often pries
beneath the relationships connecting artist, curator, gallerist
and patron, proposing an entirely new thematic and visual
meaning for the creation of art. Asher's interventions articulate
their historical time and allocated exhibition period, almost
always denying artworks both permanence and transcendence; as
such, when not kept in 'public storage' as part of a collection, his
interventions can be historicised through documentation only.

Kunsthalle Bern, 1992 evolved from Asher's early explorations
of institutional space and display during the late 1960s and
early 70s. A key example of these is *Claire Copley Gallery, Inc.,
Los Angeles, California, U.S.A., September 21—October 12, 1974*
(1974; fig.17), which, following *Galleria Toselli, Milan, Italy,
September 13—October 8, 1973* almost exactly a year after, also
utilised the entire exhibition area. For this work, Asher removed
the free-standing partition that blocked the rear section of the
gallery from view, so that visitors to the exhibition were made
privy to the gallery's back-room office and storage space. With
the exposure of the gallery's daily operations, viewers could
witness the normally concealed activity — the owner at her desk
(with or without clients) and paintings stacked against the wall
(awaiting sale or collection) — as part of the work. Additionally,
and in contrast, they could observe street activity through the
large 'picture' window at the gallery's entrance. Denuded of

traditional paintings and sculptures, the Claire Copley
exhibition laid bare its own economic underpinnings as well
as those of the gallery. In Asher's words, 'just as the work served
as a model of how the gallery operated, it also served as a model
for its own economic reproduction'.[34] Clearly, *Claire Copley
Gallery* presaged *Kunsthalle Bern, 1992* by embodying its own
physical setting, if on a much less complex scale than at the
Kunsthalle, where the relocation and reconnection of the heating
system throughout an entire building involved far more logisti-
cally than the removal of a single wall partition in a relatively
small gallery space. But while the *Claire Copley Gallery* project
eliminated the separation between public and private space,
or at least made the space of management and commerce visible
to 'anyone', for *Kunshalle Bern, 1992* his intervention left
untouched the office spaces.[35]

A few years later, *Stedelijk Van Abbemuseum, Eindhoven,
Netherlands, August 3—August 29, 1977* (1977) took place
(spatially and temporarily) above the gridded ceilings of
the Van Abbemuseum's 1930s wing. Anticipating Asher's
employment of radiators in the Bern installation, the Eindhoven
work used the existing functional features of the museum
building to material advantage. In this case, Asher utilised the
rectangular, translucent, glass ceiling panels that, resting just
below the roof on a metal grid, diffused light into the galleries.
The exhibition occurred in half of the museum's ten original
galleries, which are symmetrically contained within a square
ground plan.[36] On a handout, Asher described how he integrated
the diffusers into an exhibition that 'became … its own
subject',[37] declaring:

> *I propose that before the exhibition opens on August 3,
> all the glass ceiling panels in rooms 1, 2, 3 and 4 plus all
> the glass ceiling panels up to the centre row in rooms 5 and*

The duration of the exhibition was then defined by the time
it took the installation crew, working overhead before public
hours in galleries emptied of all other artworks, to return
the panels to their original positions. During the 27-day span,
traditional objects selected by the director filled the other
half of the museum. Based on the fact that installing artworks
commonly requires hiring temporary labour, Asher staged a
work that turned this general practice into the exhibition itself.
Rather than leaving routinely unseen preparations and persons
contributing to a finished display out of the picture, Asher made
the time and effort carried out by others the centre of the work.
Featuring manual labour, *Stedelijk Van Abbemuseum* dispensed
with the fashioning of 'finished', static, signed and transportable
objects brought about solely by way of an artist's authorial 'hand'
— a thread that, as mentioned earlier, runs through all his work.
Rather than viewing artworks on walls or in ambulatory space,
visitors to the Van Abbemuseum during Asher's exhibition had
to look up at the ceiling in order to follow the incremental
unfolding day by day of the reinstallation of the diffusers.
Somewhat similarly in Bern a decade and a half later, viewers
would traverse the sum of the exhibition rooms devoted to a
single installation. However visually disparate, and despite
the chronological nature of the Eindhoven piece, both works had
the same material basis: both were fabricated out of functional
structural elements belonging to the buildings in which they
took place.

To a similarly singular effect, Asher again employed existing architectural elements in *The Museum of Contemporary Art, Chicago, Illinois, U.S.A., June 8—August 12, 1979* (1979). This work shares an obvious affiliation with the Bern installation because both dismantled a given architectural feature within the institution's premises while proposing a double negation of the language of modernist architecture and Minimal sculpture. The work for the MCA responded to the institution's newly expanded exhibition facility and the board's accompanying decision to embark on acquiring a permanent collection. A decade earlier, in preparation for the museum's opening in 1967, the architects of the newly remodelled, single-story Ontario Street building, the architectural practice Brenner, Danforth, Rockwell, had covered the brick façade with stucco. Booth, Nagle & Hartray, the firm in charge of the subsequent renovation and extension in 1979, was faced with the task of connecting the existing building to an adjoining, gutted, three-story brownstone. The architects expanded the original building by adding a trussed second-floor gallery — named the Bergman Gallery — that further augmented the exhibition space while providing a passage between the previously separate structures. Of major note, they also covered the buildings on either side of the trussed gallery with a grid of brushed-aluminium cladding (each panel based on a module with an area of approximately half a square metre).

Commissioned for the permanent collection, Asher's MCA work attended to the Bergman Gallery, which also featured windows overlooking the street. As he wrote on an explanatory handout, this space 'functions as a showcase so that art is visible from the street'.[39] Before the completion of the museum's new building, he had arranged for two rows of the exterior metal panels to be hinged for temporary removal and installation on the wall of the Bergman Gallery (fig.22). As he pointed out, 'the ten panels from the east side of the building and the eight from the west are arranged inside so that they correspond exactly to their previous positions outside'.[40] The resulting 9-metre-wide empty space between the double row of panels could be used to show the work of another artist without interrupting the impact of the abutted, modular, aluminium squares, with their sleek, uniform, reductive, industrial surfaces (fig.24).[41] Once the piece was no longer on display and the panels were reattached to the building's exterior, the work became, in Asher's words, 'stored in full public view', rather than in a warehouse as a traditional art object would be (fig.23). Alternatively, when shown within the context of the Bergman Gallery, the large metallic squares shed their architectural function as a decorative, exterior overlay to be perceived as an artwork. But, like the Kunsthalle Bern installation, the essential relation of the work to the institution led to its disappearance when the museum moved out of its original building on Ontario Street to a newly designed building on Chicago Avenue in 1996.[42] Here the 'fragility', in a sense, of Asher's works becomes especially apparent with regard to exhibitions that are most intimately associated with institutions: they are at the mercy of the structural changes within the context they act upon and remain subject to permanent dismantling in most instances.

Once again Asher brought context to bear on the content of his work when he was invited to participate in 'Heute' ('Today'), a corollary exhibition included as the conclusion of the large-scale project 'Westkunst' ('Western Art') in Cologne in 1981. Modelled on Cologne's grand tradition of early twentieth-century exhibitions that looked toward the future of art, 'Westkunst', curated by a team under the direction of Kasper König, was ambitiously billed as a comprehensive examination of modern art from 1939 to 1981. Like 'Sunderbund' (1912), 'Werkbund' (1914) and 'Pressa' (1928), 'Westkunst' was held in the Staatenhaus, on the city's fairgrounds, which accommodated

the more than 800 artworks included in the show. 'Westkunst'
gave a perspective on present-day art in terms of the movements
of preceding decades, proposing many historical groupings
as subsets to overarching categories: 'Weltkrieg und Moderne'
('World War and Modernity'), 'Abstraktion als Weltsprache'
('Abstraction as a Universal Language') and 'Zwischen
Fortschritt und Verweigerung' ('Between Progress and Refusal').[43]

The organisation of 'Heute' was entrusted to the Cologne dealer
Rudolph Zwirner, who invited private galleries to fill sixteen
allocated spaces with objects by artists of his choice.[44] What
such an historical narrative and the effects its linear structure
and its conclusion in a commercial environment might have
for understanding individual works of art was the subject of
Asher's contribution. His work, titled *Westkunst, Köln, Germany,
'Heute', May 29—August 16, 1981* (1981), commented on the
tendency of public exhibitions to serve as venues for private
commercial transactions, especially evidenced by the attempt
to legitimise art of the day in terms of art of the past while
presenting it as a commodity available for purchase. He did this
by creating an ironic reversal of the organisational structure of
'Heute'. Asher was the only artist without representation (his
participation was directly solicited by König), and, therefore,
his work was not destined for sale. Installed in the entryway
that flanked the two opposite doorways bridging 'Heute' and
'Westkunst', Asher's work consisted of eight variously shaped
chairs on four carpeted platforms (fig.26). The chairs were
those he had requested for loan from the participating galleries,
eight of which had complied: Galerie Hans Mayer, Galerie
Konrad Fischer and Galerie Arno Kohnen from Düsseldorf;
Paula Cooper Gallery from New York; Galerie Nächst St.
Stephan from Vienna; Galerie Rüdiger Schöttle from Munich;
Galerie Pablo Stähli from Zurich; and Galleria Lucio Amelio
from Naples.

Asher distributed the chairs among the four platforms: one held
three, two others exhibited two chairs each and the final
stand presented a lone seat. Each chair had its own formal
characteristics and, like the Bern radiators, conveyed both a
sculptural and a design aspect in their mode of display. A wall
label described Asher's methodology for the installation:

> *My work is designed for an exhibition that seeks to critically
> analyse art production. The 'Today' exhibition has been
> economically supported not only by the general public but
> also by private interests, mainly commercial galleries.*
>
> *Each of the exhibition areas has been sponsored by a separate
> private interest, which has resulted in a hybridisation of
> the Art Fair and Museum setting.*
>
> *The chairs used in this work, usually meant for visitor
> seating, were lent by the private commercial galleries
> represented in 'Westkunst'.*[45]

The most salient feature of Asher's work was the role reversal it
initiated. Instead of being invited by a gallery to take part in the
exhibition, he, as artist, invited all the galleries to take part in
the construction of his work. Unlike paintings, sculptures or
installation pieces destined for the market, Asher's contribution
to 'Heute' represented an investment in aesthetic production and
reception without ensuing financial reward. Like Duchampian
readymades (and the Bern radiators), the chairs were taken from
a context of everyday use. Unlike a now-sacrosanct readymade,
however, the chairs — borrowed temporarily — were returned
to the galleries to function once more as utilitarian objects.[46]
Interior wall partitions built into exhibition spaces came into
play in Asher's exhibitions of the 1980s, as they had previously
on occasions when he featured them, not as neutral backdrops,

but as the components of a finished work. In 1988, he responded
to the newly refurbished exhibition area at Artists Space
in New York with *Artists Space, "Michael Asher/James Coleman,"
New York, June 2—July 2, 1988* (1988) dealt with the pretence
of renovation that allows architecture to vie with art as a
dominating physical presence rather than simply playing
a (literally) supporting role. For his part in a two-person
exhibition with James Coleman, Asher restored the space,
to some degree, to its previous condition, by cancelling out the
protruding sculptural aspect of added walls that paralleled the
gallery's outer shell. He did this by vertically extending partial
walls, to bring them up to meet the ceiling.[47] Leaving the
extensions unpainted, he signalled the division between art-as-
architecture and architecture that mimics sculptural three-
dimensionality. While the walls of the Kunsthalle Bern
remained bare during Asher's exhibition, only partially occupied
by hot-water pipes, the walls of Artists Space provided the work
with a material existence that likewise availed itself of, in order
to cite, its own site.

All these works are directly comparable to *Kunsthalle Bern, 1992*
because they physically engaged with existing architecture and
with utilitarian objects belonging or relevant to the specific
site. As with the removed partition at Claire Copley Gallery,
the walls at Artists Space reverted to their previous state at the
end of the exhibition.[48]

Asher's 1983 work for the exhibition 'In Context', organised
by the Museum of Contemporary Art, Los Angeles and held
in the Geffen Contemporary (formerly called the Temporary
Contemporary), prefigured *Kunsthalle Bern, 1992* in a less obvious
way.[49] Instead of employing architectural features of the museum
or functional objects, the work for 'In Context' took an alternative tack in its use of language to address its contextual situation.

On the main entryway column facing visitors as they came into
to the unusually large exhibition area, Asher hung, from edge-
to-edge, a thin, square, plexiglas plaque at eye level. The plaque,
bright orange in colour, stood out as a vibrant backdrop for white
lettering that read 'The Michael Asher Lobby' in two lines of
lettering. Additionally, he designed a small card measuring 5
by 9 centimetres when creased in the middle. Its white lettering
on the same orange background echoed the plaque on the column.
Placed on the information desk in the reception area, it provided
visitors with a printed text on its inside while offering itself
as a souvenir. The white-on-orange text spelt out the artist's
proposal to MOCA, requesting

> *that an agreement be made which will give me a license
> for the aesthetic control of the lobby of the Museum. In so
> doing, the Museum will then sublicense this area making it
> possible to be rented from me on a monthly basis [...] During
> the license period, however, maintenance, insurance
> and taxes will be at the Museum's expense, a responsibility
> generally assumed by the Museum for the works that they
> house. I have requested that they regulate all day-to-day
> functions and operations of the lobby area without my
> intervention.*

Laying claim, through payment, to the lobby area of MOCA,
where donors' names are featured along the entryway wall,
facing visitors, Asher inverted the usual relationship between
artist and institution. 'The Michael Asher Lobby' drew attention
to art's normally unacknowledged dependence on real estate,
as well as on the financial support of patrons whose names
are routinely exhibited in museum lobbies. It thus succeeded in
bypassing the traditional process of making an arrangement of
objects by making an 'arrangement' in the form of an agreement
instead. Despite its deliberate lack of volumetric materiality and

demonstrable physical presence, the MOCA work presaged
Kunsthalle Bern, 1992 in its abstract embodiment of its
institutional — and, here, invisible — space. Rather than taking
form within an exhibition space, 'The Michael Asher Lobby'
was based on an artist's offer to a museum to make a monetary
exchange that would constitute the work. It demonstrated
Asher's profound recognition (turned to aesthetic purpose)
of the invisible socio-economic systems and transactions
that sustain institutions. Following from such a recognition,
the Bern Kunsthalle's radiators and heating pipes visibly
objectified, by paradigmatically picturing, the otherwise unseen
mechanisms that endow (financially as well as physically)
museums and galleries with their lifeblood.

Using the Museum's Collection
For his participation in several group exhibitions organised by
museums in the late 1970s and early 80s, Asher, in three instances
— twice at the Art Institute of Chicago (1979 and 1982) and once
at the Los Angeles County Museum of Art (1981) — utilised art
objects belonging to the venue's permanent collection. These
three works fall within the category of Asher's work involving
installations that incorporate artworks belonging to specific
museums. They relate to *Kunsthalle Bern, 1992* inasmuch as
the artist turned to objects already available in the museum,
although, of course, as works of art themselves they were
not part of the architectural structure of the building (such
as radiators, partition walls or external cladding). Asher's
first piece at the Art Institute was part of the 73rd American
Exhibition in 1979, which presented work by sixteen artists.[50]
Avoiding the space devoted to the temporary exhibition, Asher
instead removed a life-size, weathered, bronze statue of George
Washington from its longstanding place under the central
arch of the museum's façade to the centre of Gallery 219 (fig.25).
At the time, this gallery — a relatively small, almost square

space painted greyish teal — displayed the Art Institute's permanent collection of eighteenth-century European painting, sculpture and decorative art. The objects were placed symmetrically around the room, and the paintings were beside and above one another nearly to the ceiling, to evoke a period-style installation. As indicated by a printed text guiding visitors from the 73rd American Exhibition on the main floor up to the permanent collection galleries on the second level, Asher claimed:

> *In this work I am interested in the way the sculpture* [of George Washington] *functions when it is viewed in its 18th-century context instead of in its prior relationship to the façade of the building.* [...] *Once inside of Gallery 219 the sculpture can be seen in connection with the ideas of other European works of the same period.*[51]

A fairly mediocre, early twentieth-century cast of a white marble sculpture by the French sculptor Jean-Antoine Houdon that is located in the rotunda of the Virginia State Capitol, *George Washington* (1785—91; cast 1917) 'fit' with its eighteenth-century surroundings historically and stylistically, while leaving a path for continued visitor circulation around the room. Yet, it also subtly sounded a discordant, even humorous, note because of its weathered appearance and the warlike posturing of its subject, whom Houdon portrayed with aggrandising intent. Dressed as a leader of the American Revolutionary War, the first president of the United States holds a sword in one hand while the other rests on a bundle of fasces indicative of ancient (and outmoded) pomp and circumstance.[52]

Asher's relocation of the bronze cast of George Washington functioned on a number of levels by calling attention to unspoken modes of perception incurred by contextual conditions that differ

inside and outside of museum walls — conditions that allowed
the Kunsthalle Bern's radiators and hot-water pipes (and
the MCA's cladding) to replace the traditional materials of
sculpture. Equally, his moving of *George Washington* erased any
division between the statue and its contextual setting insofar
as the work fused with its eighteenth-century environment to
become an aesthetic — as well as enterable — entity. As Asher
also noted in the handout,

> [In the process] *of locating the sculpture within its own
> time frame in Gallery 219, I am placing it within the
> framework of a contemporary exhibition, through my
> participation in that exhibition.*

While the work was on view in connection with the 73rd
American Exhibition, Gallery 219 continued to display the Art
Institute's permanent collection, in its usual chronological and
geographical arrangement. As for the bronze cast — a reminder
of the traditionally disconnected, autonomous object — it acted
as a catalyst for an artwork that drew its content from the
statue's treatment according to curatorial installation practices
rather than as a commemorative object decoratively gracing
the museum's exterior.[53]

Three years later, as part of the 74th American Exhibition,[54]
Asher created a work based on two paintings in the museum's
permanent collection. At his request, the curatorial department
enlisted viewers to stand for a short duration of roughly thirty
minutes every day in front of one of two paintings in Gallery 226:
Nu assis dans une baignoire (*Nude Seated in a Bathtub*, 1910) by
Marcel Duchamp and *Daniel-Henry Kahnweiler* (1910) by Pablo
Picasso.[55] Asher also produced a handout — directing visitors
from the entrance of the lower-level galleries that held the
American Exhibition upstairs to Gallery 226 — in which he

indicated the disparity between the degrees to which the
paintings had been reproduced in books. Both were executed
in the same year by two giants of modern art, but while the
Duchamp painting had been reproduced in nine publications,
the Picasso had appeared in fifty. On the handout, Asher also
offered the rationale behind his project:

> *Supposedly conveying knowledge of artistic production,
> reproduction paradoxically tends to colour or interfere
> with the first-hand experience of the original work of art.
> With reference to the full cycle of aesthetic production
> and cultural reception, the viewers serve to demonstrate
> the museum visitor's role at the point of presentation. [...]
> When my work is on view museum visitors are able to
> witness the completion of the viewing process while actively
> being engaged in this process themselves.*

The enlisted viewers did not act out their role in any
demonstrably performative way. They simply stood in an
attentive and relaxed manner beside one another as they looked
at the paintings, which they bracketed with their bodies,
but did not block. Standard, cardboard wall labels, like those
used by the museum to provide didactic information about any
object, identified the paintings as part of Asher's work for the
American Exhibition.

The installation took cognisance of the fact that the same
institutions that make artworks available are also those that
provide (and market) photographic reproductions in publications
or, in more recent times, on computer and mobile telephone
screens. With this in mind, Asher's work reproduced, without
mechanical or technological intervention, the process of viewing
art as an unadulterated physical and mental activity that takes
place in museums. With the idea of dismantling barriers to

direct experience, he exhibited the viewing of art in the context
of concrete and institutional actuality by embodying hired
viewers to give material and thematic form to a work about
witnessing the act of perceptual engagement with art.

*Los Angeles Museum of Contemporary Art (LACMA), Los Angeles,
California, U.S.A., "The Museum as Site: Sixteen Artists — Seventeen
Projects", July 16—October 4, 1981* (1981) comprised three
physically separate elements: *The Kentuckian* (1954), a Thomas
Hart Benton painting on display in the museum's permanent
collection; a carved wood sign; and a poster designed by Asher
for the museum's outdoor stanchions for exhibition publicity.
Together these components pertained to the museum as a
place for housing a public art collection and, in this case,
as an institution that is located in Hancock Park, next to
the prehistoric La Brea Tar Pits. With these three elements,
Asher created an installation that connected the interior and
exterior of the museum and, in so doing, extended the work's
thematic reach from the permanent collection galleries to the
neighbouring park. The work was sparked by Asher's observation
that the carved wood sign usually at the park's entrance (near
Wilshire Boulevard, on the path between LACMA's B. Gerald
Cantor Sculpture Garden and the tar pits) was missing from
its post in the ground. He requested that the sign, stating the
county ordinance 'Dogs Must Be Kept On Leash', be reinstated.
The sign, as it so happened, alluded to the imagery of Benton's
painting, which depicts a youthful, towering man carrying
a rifle and camping gear, accompanied by a boy and a dog,
set against the sky as he strides across the rugged terrain of a
stylised mountainous landscape.

The poster designed by Asher and displayed in the outdoor
stanchions, while indirectly related to the county's wood sign,
had more definitive ties to Benton's painting. At the top of the

poster, under his own name rendered in a typeface often associated with Hollywood films, Asher affixed a colour lobby card for the film *The Kentuckian* (1955), co-produced, directed by and starring Burt Lancaster; at the bottom, Asher placed the original black-and-white production still of the same image. In between the lobby card and the still, he inserted a photographic reproduction of *Guide to the Features, Trees and Shrubs of Hancock Park (with notes on the Indian uses of the native plants)*, a foldout pamphlet available to visitors of the neighbouring George C. Page Museum, which is dedicated to the excavation and preservation of fossils from the tar pits. Underneath the guide, Asher included his own text directing people to his work in 'The Museum as Site: Sixteen Projects', which he described as

> *the reinstallation of the county sign on the path between the B.G. Cantor Sculpture Garden and the lake pit adjacent to Wilshire Boulevard in Hancock Park. The painting* The Kentuckian *by Thomas Hart Benton is part of the permanent collection of the Los Angeles County Museum of Art.*[56]

Benton's painting was, in fact, a gift to the museum from Lancaster, who acquired the canvas because it had been commissioned (although not used) by the production studio for the film. The image on the lobby card and film still, found by Asher, represents a man — accompanied by a woman, a boy and a dog — emerging from a path in the woods, the dog tugging at its leash in advance of the group. In the film, based on Felix Holt's 1951 novel *The Gabriel Horn* and set in the 1820s, Lancaster plays a frontiersman from Kentucky who becomes embroiled with two women as he makes his way with his son from Kentucky to Texas to seek his fortune. Riding roughshod across wide-open spaces and battling Native Americans, Lancaster overcomes all manner of obstacles.

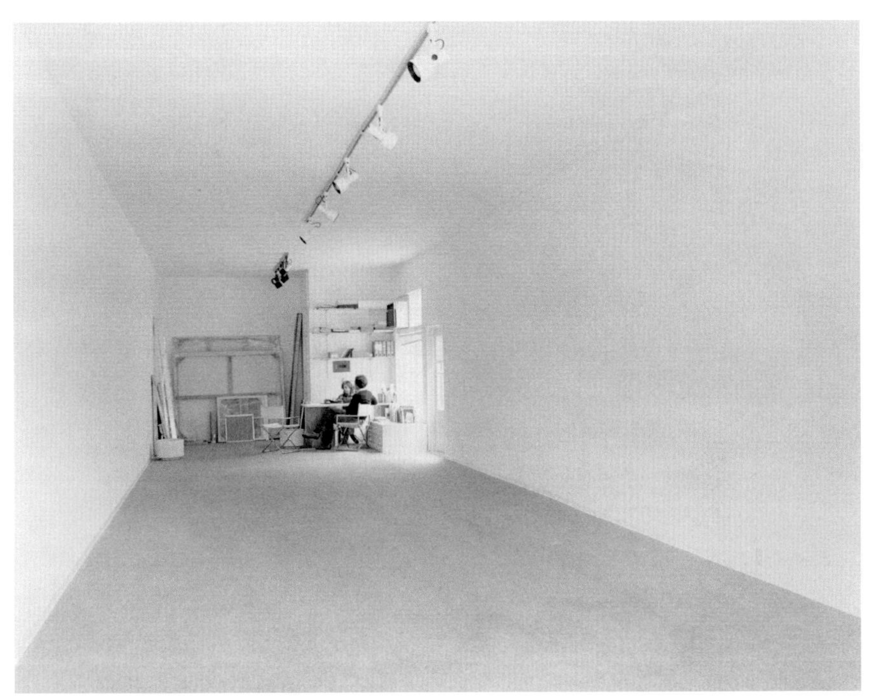

17. Michael Asher,
Claire Copley Gallery, Inc.,
Los Angeles, California, U.S.A.,
September 21—October 12, 1974, 1974,
installation at Claire Copley Gallery
view through the gallery towards the
office and storage areas
Photograph: Gary Kruger

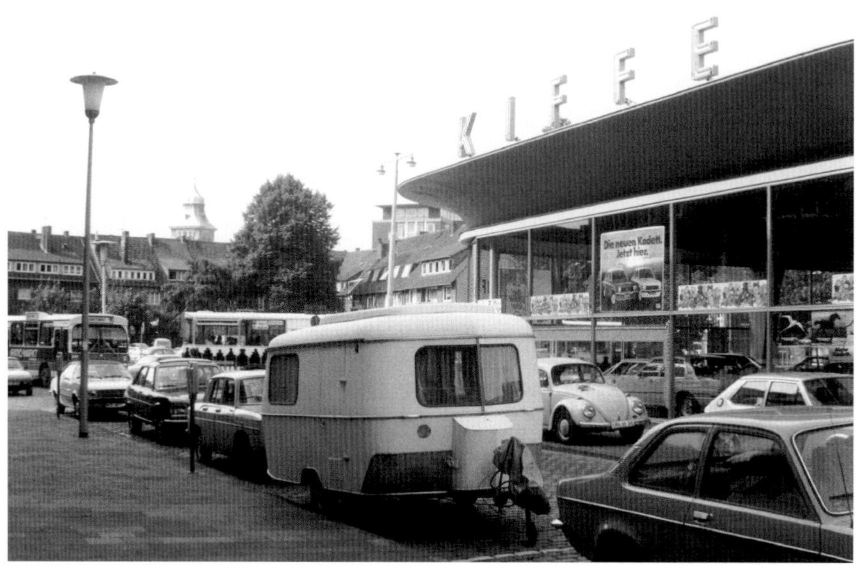

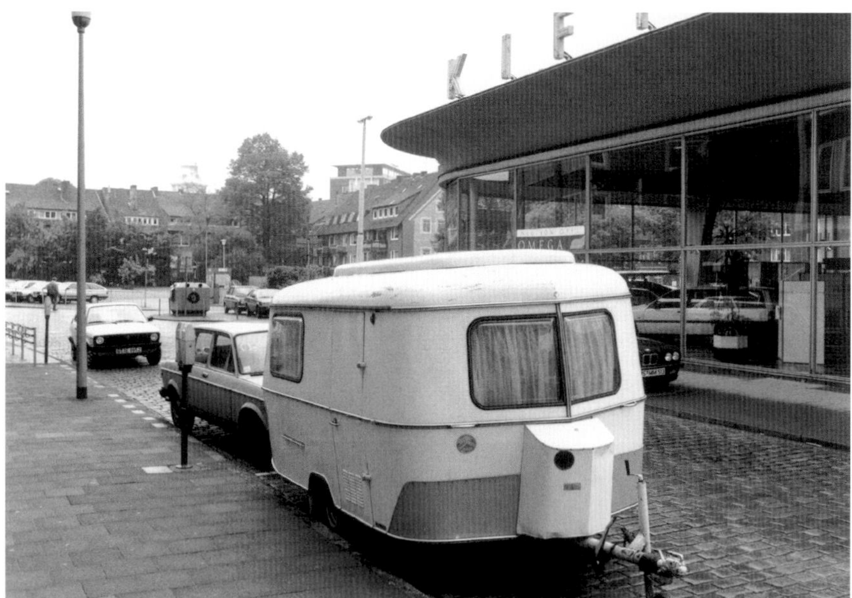

18. Michael Asher, *Westfälisches
Landesmuseum für Kunst und Kulturgeschichte,
Münster, Germany, 'Skulptur',
July 3—November 13, 1977*, 1977,
4th week, Alter Steinweg, across from
Kiffe-Pavillon, parking metre no.274 or 275
Photograph: Roudolf Wakonigg /WLMKuK

19. Michael Asher, *Westfälisches
Landesmuseum für Kunst und Kulturgeschichte,
Münster, Germany, 'Skulptur',
June 14—October 4, 1987*, 1987,
4th week, Alter Steinweg, across from
Kiffe-Pavillon, parking metre no.2,200
Photograph: Roudolf Wakonigg /WLMKuK

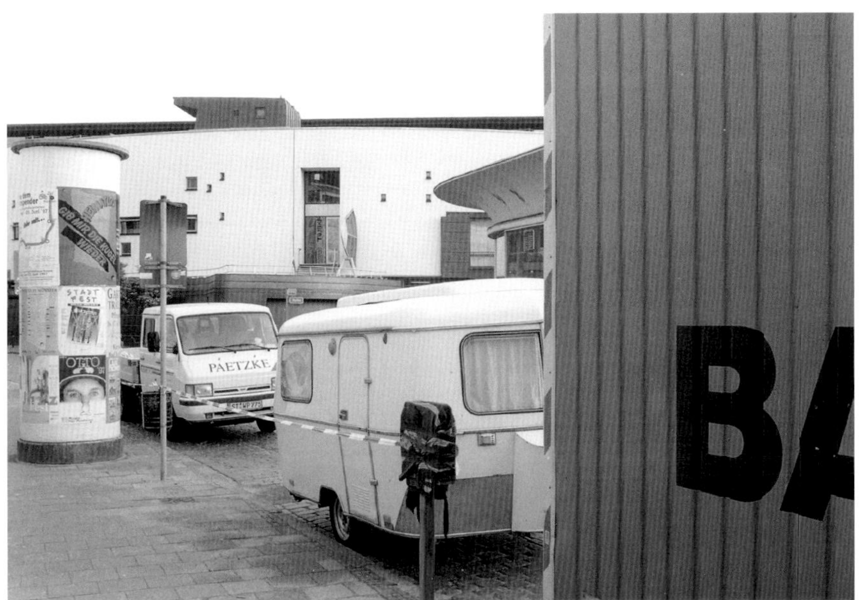

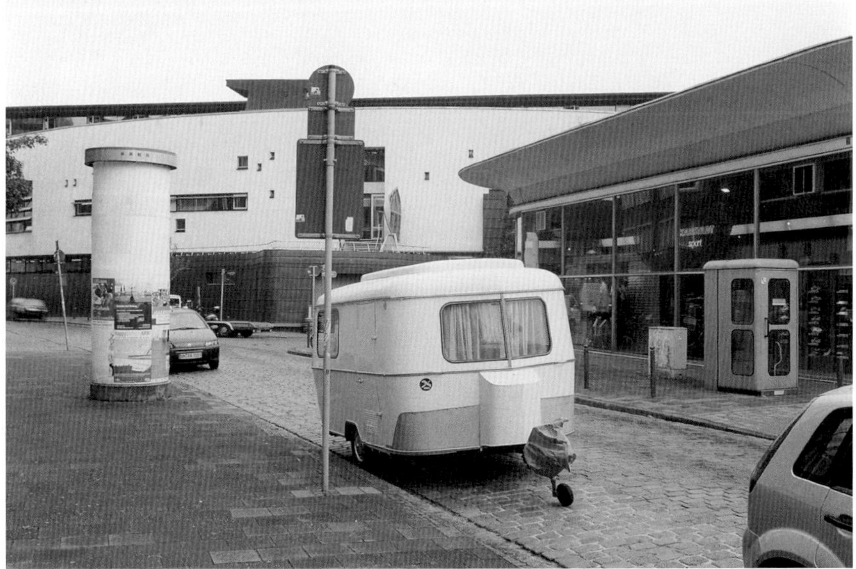

20. Michael Asher, *Westfälisches Landesmuseum für Kunst und Kulturgeschichte, Münster, Germany, 'Skulptur Projekte Münster 1997', June 22—September 28, 1997*, 1997, 4th week, Alter Steinweg, across from Kiffe-Pavillon, parking metre no.2,560
Photograph: Roman Mensing

21. Michael Asher, *Westfälisches Landesmuseum für Kunst und Kulturgeschichte, Münster, Germany, 'Sculpture Projects Münster 07', June 17—September 30, 2007*, 2007, 4th week, Alter Steinweg, across from Kiffe-Pavillon
Photograph: Roman Mensing

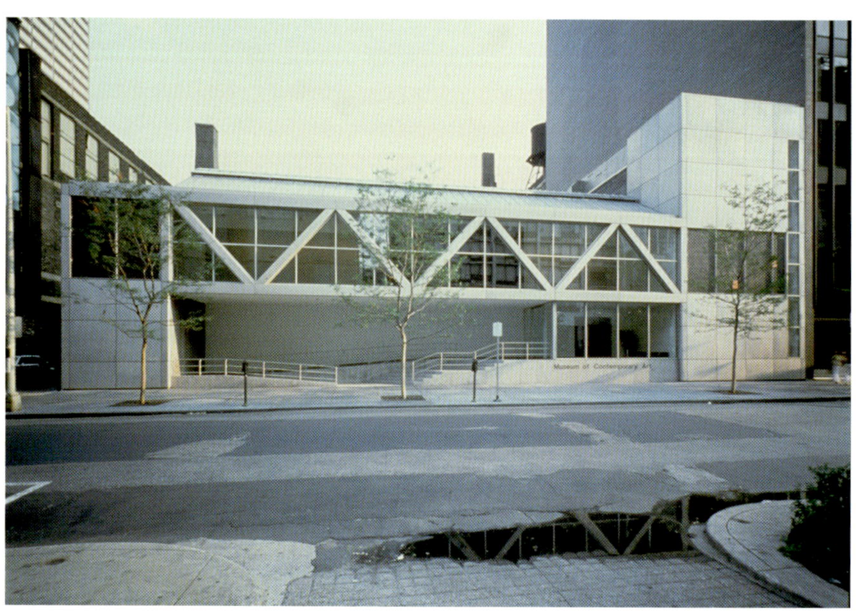

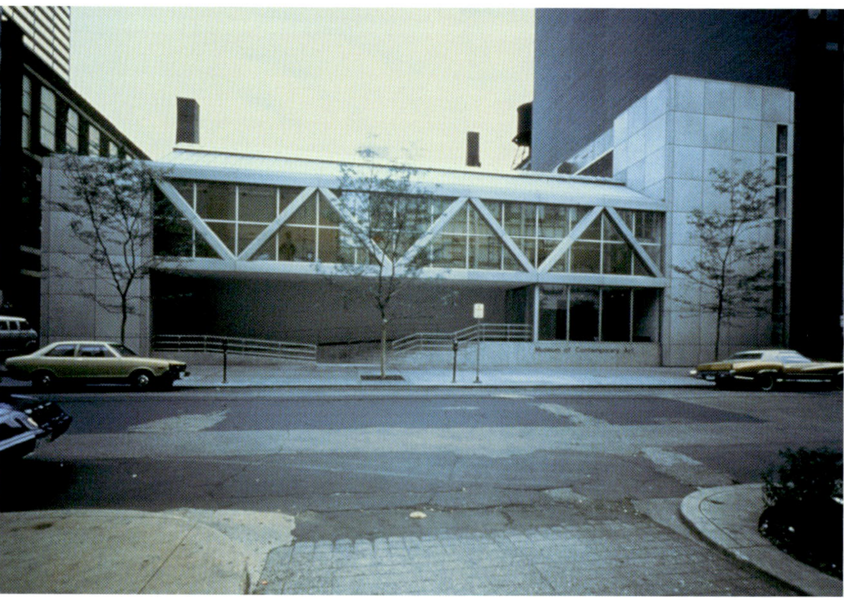

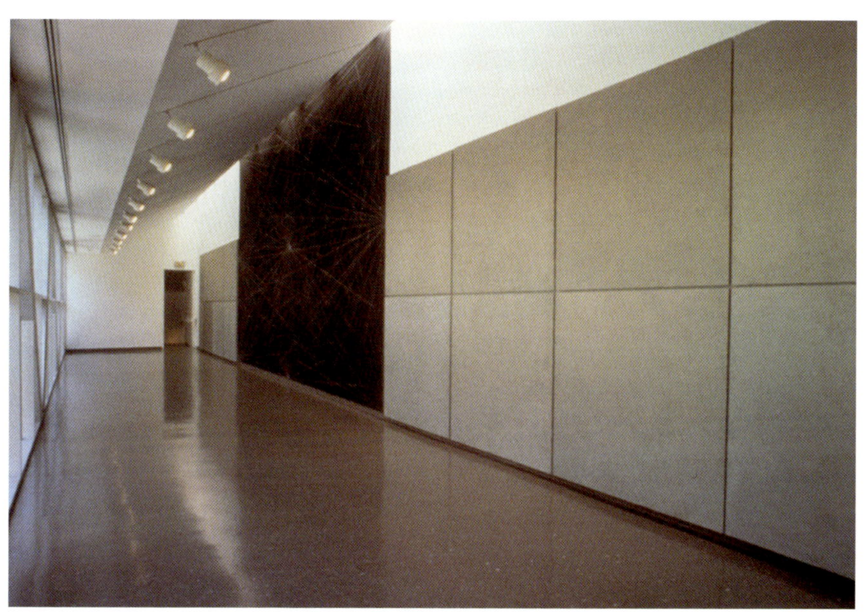

22. Michael Asher,
*The Museum of Contemporary Art, Chicago,
Illinois, U.S.A., June 8—August 12, 1979*, 1979,
façade of the MCA during the exhibition
Courtesy MCA, Chicago

23. Michael Asher,
*The Museum of Contemporary Art, Chicago,
Illinois, U.S.A., June 8—August 12, 1979*, 1979,
façade of the MCA with the panels in
place and the work in public storage
Courtesy MCA, Chicago

24. Michael Asher,
*The Museum of The Museum of
Contemporary Art, Chicago, Illinois, U.S.A.,
June 8—August 12, 1979*, 1979,
installation view looking west into
the Bergman Gallery; Sol LeWitt's
*Lines from the Center of the Wall,
Four Corners, and Four Sides to Points
on a Grid* (1976) was drawn in the
available wall space between the panels
Photograph: Michael Asher
© Estate of Sol LeWitt 2012

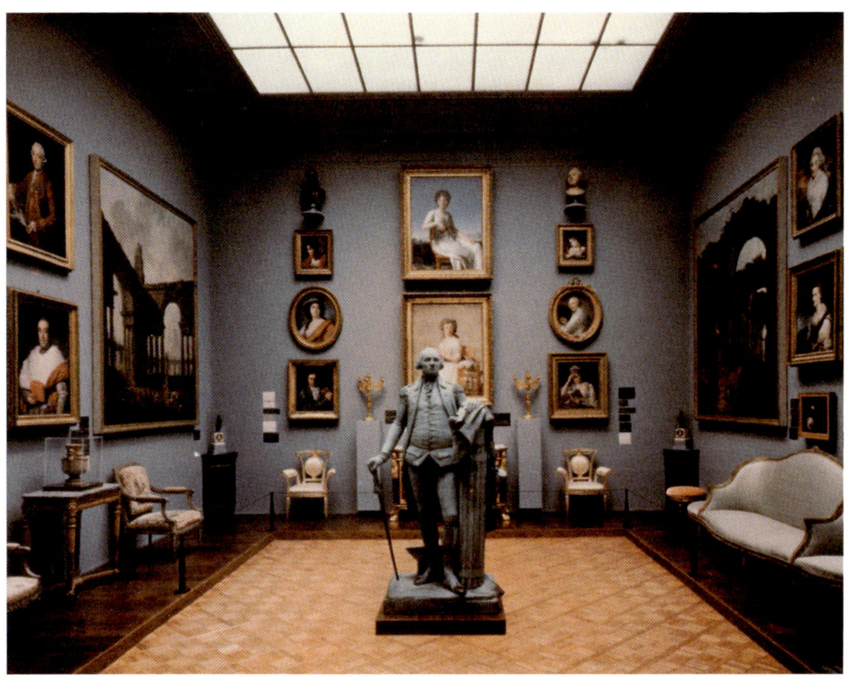

25. Michael Asher,
The Art Institute of Chicago, Chicago, Illinois, U.S.A., '73rd American Exhibition', June 9—August 5, 1979, 1979,
colour postcard of the installation in Gallery 219 published by the Art Institute of Chicago after the '73rd American Exhibition'

The caption on the reverse reads: 'The replica in bronze of *George Washington*, 1788, by Jean Antoiner Houdon, originally in front of the Michigan Avenue Entrance, can be seen in the foreground of this gallery. It was installed in an 18th century context by Michael Asher as his work in the 73rd American Exhibition.'
Photograph: Rusty Culp

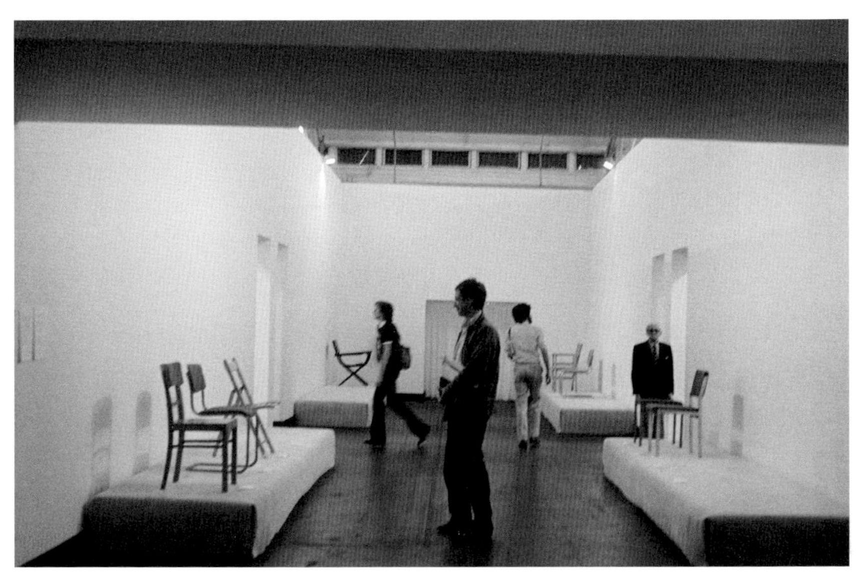

26. Michael Asher,
Westkunst, Köln, Germany, 'Heute',
May 29—August 16, 1981, 1981,
view of the centre hallway leading to the
gallery spaces; the four platforms correlated
architecturally with the four gallery spaces
Photograph: the artist

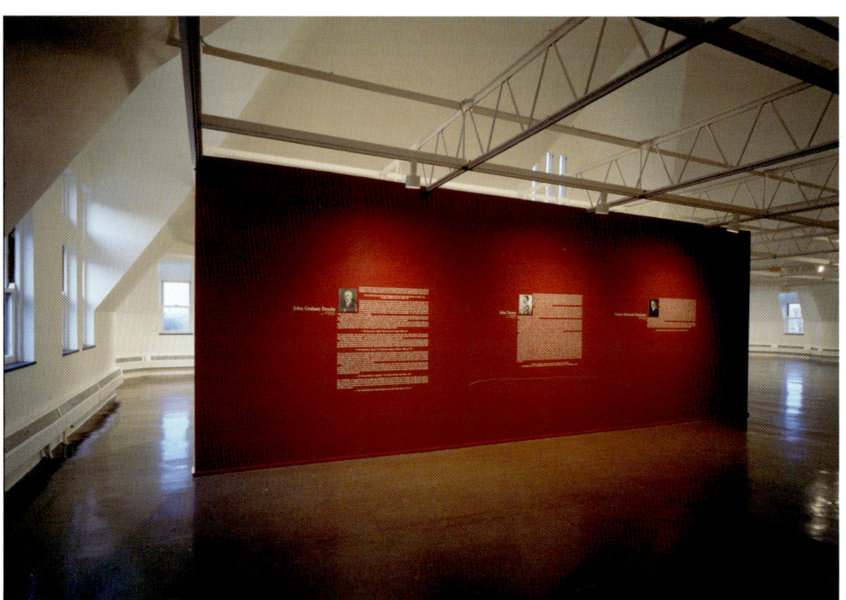

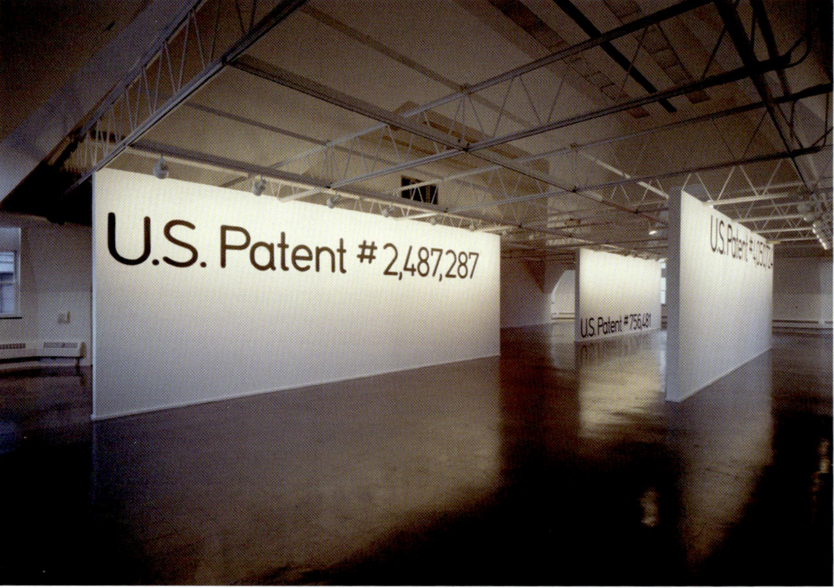

27. Michael Asher,
The Renaissance Society at the University of Chicago, Chicago, Illinois, U.S.A., January 21—March 4, 1990, 1990,
installation view, one of the three freestanding maroon walls
Photograph: Tom Van Eynde

28. Michael Asher,
The Renaissance Society at the University of Chicago, Chicago, Illinois, U.S.A., January 21—March 4, 1990, 1990,
installation view, reverse of the walls with US patent numbers
Photograph: Tom Van Eynde

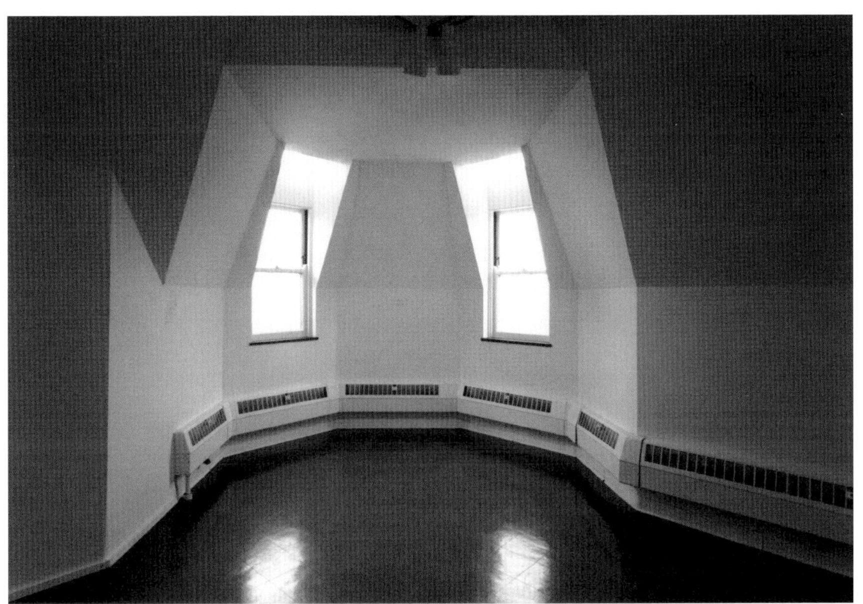

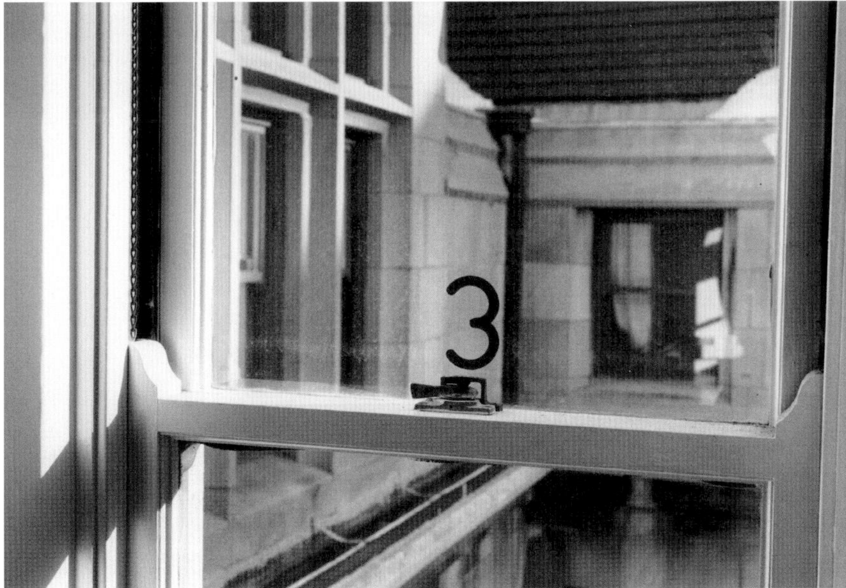

29. Michael Asher,
The Renaissance Society at the University of Chicago, Chicago, Illinois, U.S.A., January 21 — March 4, 1990, 1990, installation view of one of the three alcoves, maroon footnote 1, the window chain
Photograph: Tom Van Eynde

30. Michael Asher,
The Renaissance Society at the University of Chicago, Chicago, Illinois, U.S.A., January 21 — March 4, 1990, 1990, installation view of maroon footnote 3, the window latch
Photograph: Tom Van Eynde

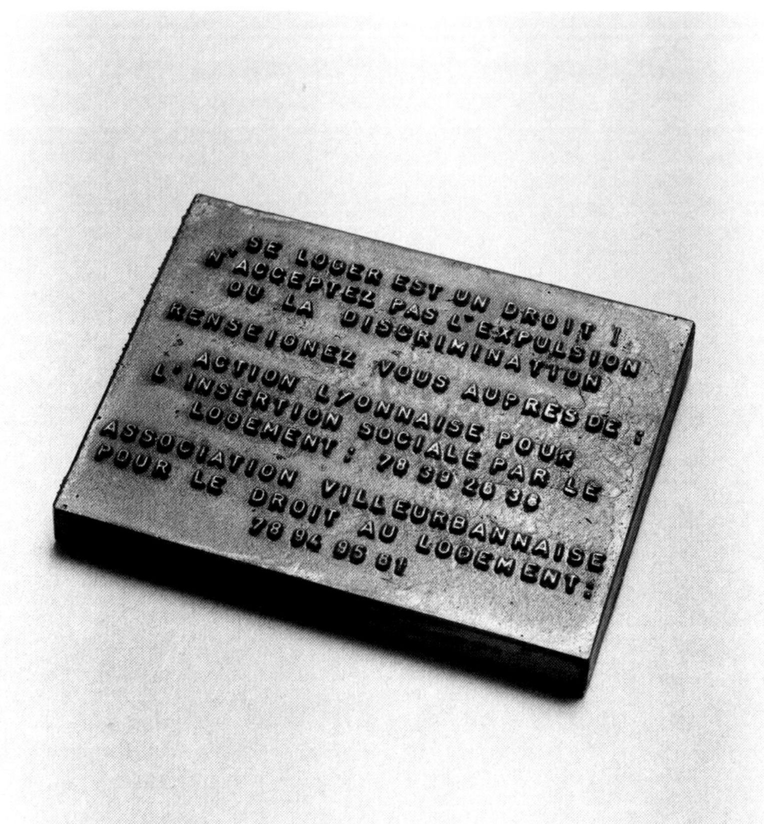

31—32. Michael Asher,
Le Nouveau Musée, Villeurbanne, France,
Opened May 22, 1991, 1991,
cast iron,
10 × 7.5cm,
thickness tapering from 1.5 to 1.1cm
Photograph: Daniel Ray

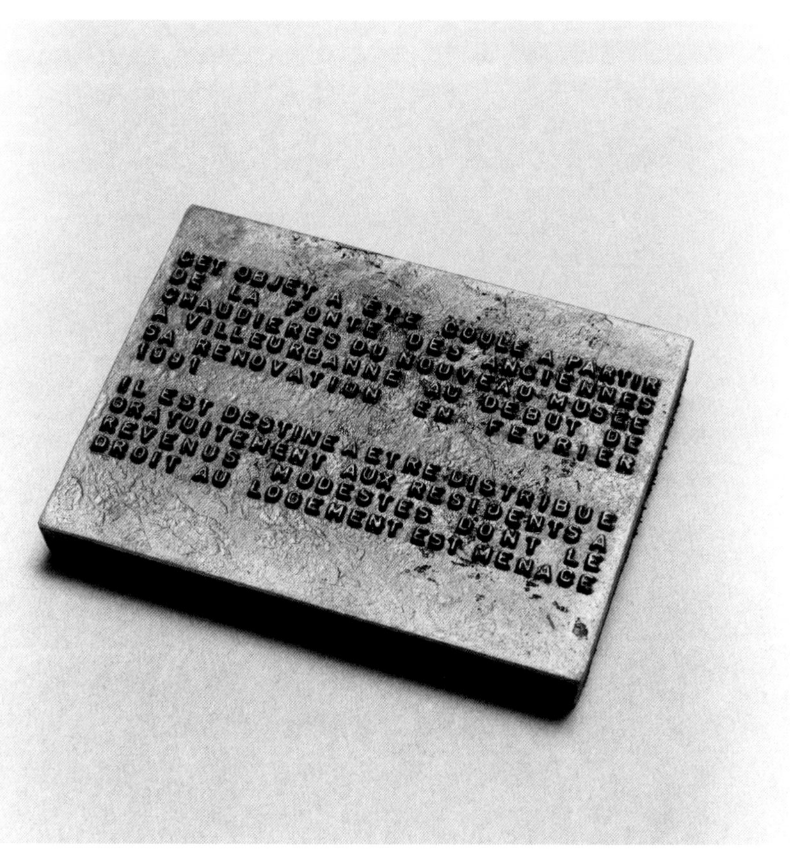

CET OBJET A ETE COULE A PARTIR
DE LA FONTE DES ANCIENNES
CHAUDIERES DU NOUVEAU MUSEE
A VILLEURBANNE AU DEBUT DE
SA RENOVATION EN FEVRIER
1991

IL EST DESTINE A ETRE REDISTRIBUE
GRATUITEMENT AUX RESIDENTS
REVENUS MODESTES DONT LE
DROIT AU LOGEMENT EST MENACE

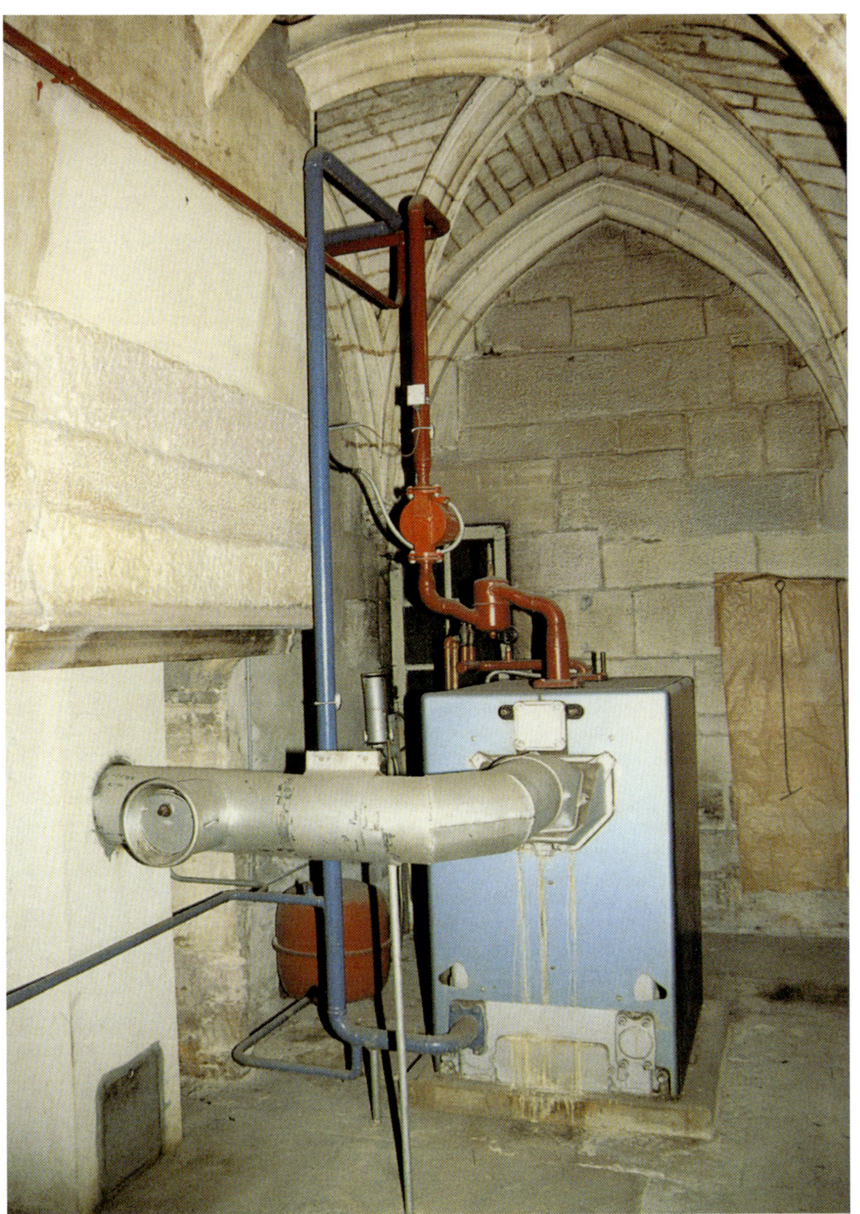

33. Michael Asher,
*Le Consortium, Dijon, France, June 7—July 27,
1991*, 1991, one of sixteen postcards produced
for the work at Le Consortium, Dijon.

The boiler in the photograph belongs to
the Hôtel Chambellan; installed in 1971,
it heats 8,640 m^3
Photograph: Pascal Pique

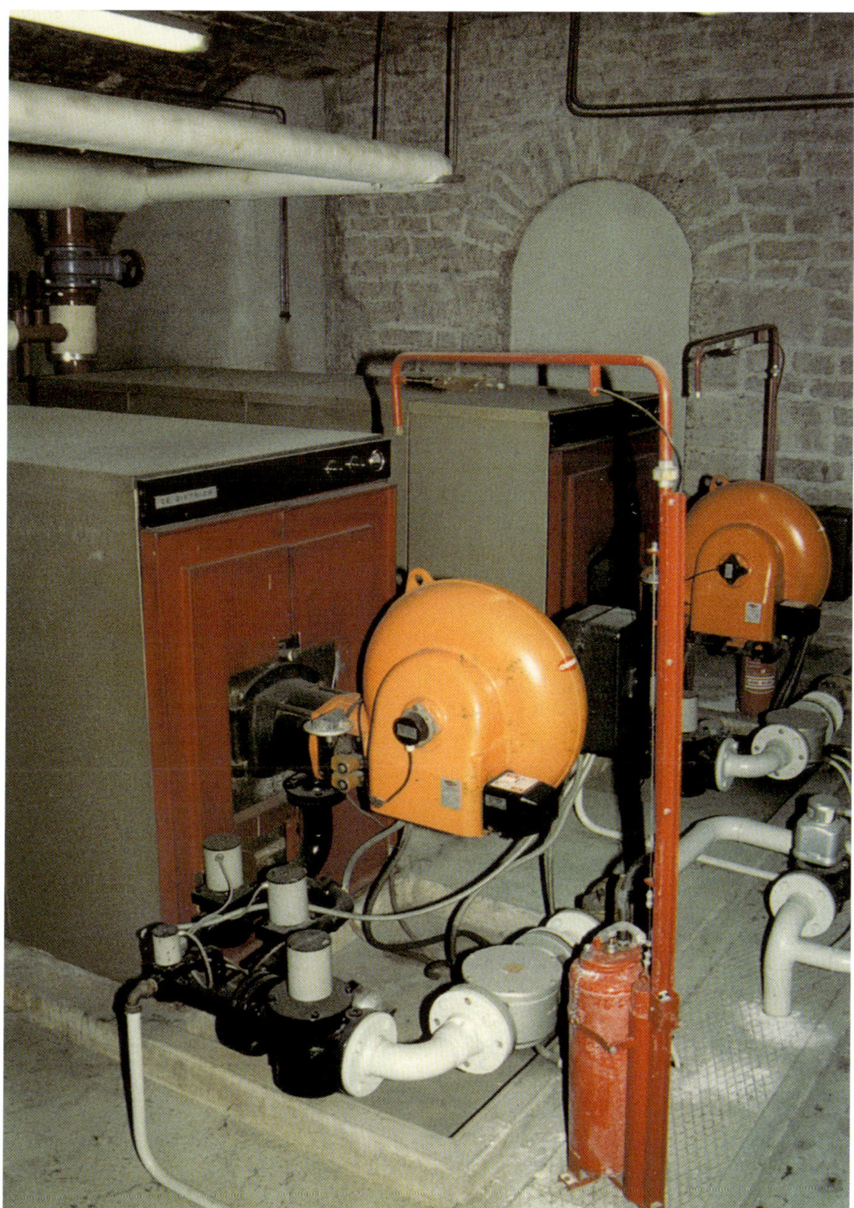

34. Michael Asher,
Le Consortium, Dijon, France, June 7 — July 27, 1991, 1991, one of sixteen postcards produced for the work at Le Consortium, Dijon.

The boiler in the photograph belongs to the Musee des Beaux-Arts; installed in 1973, it heats 2,455 m³
Photograph: Pascal Pique

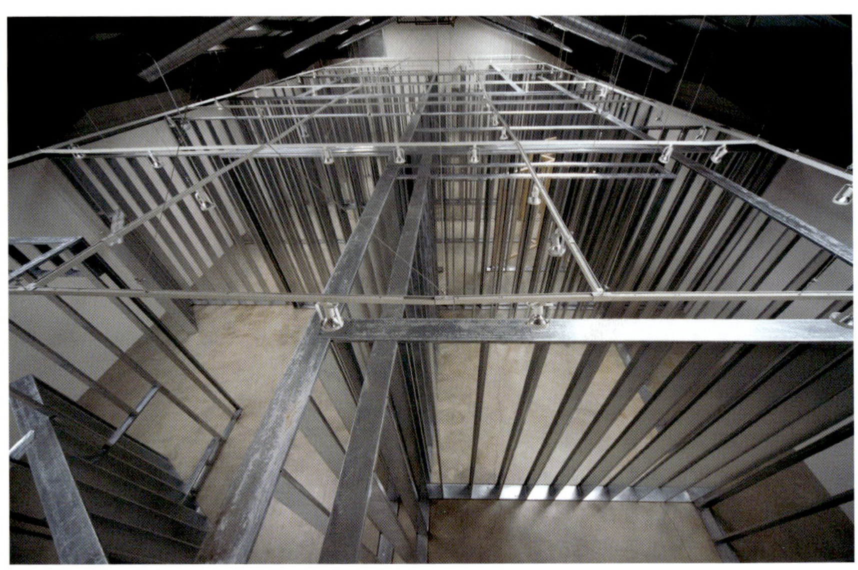

35. Michael Asher,
*Santa Monica Museum of Art, Santa Monica,
California, U.S.A., January 26—April 12,
2008*, 2008,
installation shot looking south
Photograph: Grant Mudford

Bringing together these objects and ephemera, the poster thematically linked the county sign, Benton's painting and the film. The reproduced guide to Hancock Park added yet another layer of meaning to the work on pictorial, cartographic and linguistic levels. While this guide situated visitors in relation to the park, to the museum and to Asher's work, it also provided a contrast to the lobby card and film still. Instead of participating in a fantasy narrative, typical of Hollywood adventure stories such as *The Kentuckian*, the guide presented a range of straightforward information, from telling visitors where they might be located or what destination or facility they might wish to find, to listing the Latin names for all sixty native plants along with details of their original Native American uses. Addressing the fictions in painted and moving images, Asher's LACMA work signalled the lurking threat of illusions in society that — above and beyond restrictive public ordinances and overtly manifest in the film industry — are apt to be more enthralling than they are illuminating or liberating.

Outside Architectural Confines

In the category of works by Asher that take place outside the institutional space, three of his outdoor works — in Münster (1977), Groningen (1979) and Montreal (1980) — further speak to the morphological variety of his production, which is always contingent on the purposes of an exhibition and the conditions at its site. Although these works were intended to be viewed outside of brick-and-mortar confines, all three represented institutionally based circulation and connection, although in a less concrete manner than the physical manifestation of the museum's heating system in the Bern exhibition.

In 1977, Asher, invited to participate in the first instalment of Skulptur Projekte, an exhibition organised subsequently once a decade by the Westfälisches Landesmuseum für Kunst und

Kulturgeschichte in Münster, confronted the question of
producing an outdoor sculpture without creating a discrete
or monumental object confined to one place. Throughout the
nineteen-week span of the project, Asher arranged for a small
(slightly over three-metres long), white camping trailer to
be parked in nineteen different locations across the city and
its environs.[57] The selected sites — which changed weekly
and included an alleyway, in between parked cars, outside of a
housing project and along a grassy riverbed — formed a trajectory
that moved away from the museum for the first half of the
exhibition, returning toward it during the latter half. In each
of its parked positions, the trailer, unhooked from any motor
vehicle, inserted itself — as a rounded, windowed container for
temporary occupancy — into the urban and suburban landscape
(fig.18—21). In symbiotic manner, the trailer metaphorically
attached itself to the locales in which it was successively
stationed without ultimately straying from its organisational
centre at the Landesmuseum. Figuratively grounded by the
museum — the trailer's centre of gravity — the vehicle
delineated the boundaries of an artwork that was absorbed into
the entirety of the city of Münster, within a work that critiqued
the fixed and immobile object.[58] It anticipated Asher's ensuing
revision of sculptural practice in Bern, where the work overtook
the entire Kunsthalle, albeit within an enclosed architectural
framework rather than within an open-ended urban context.

In the university town of Groningen in the Netherlands, Asher's
solo exhibition for the Stiftung Corps de Garde also materialised
in the public realm, but in a less structured fashion than
in Münster. The Groningen work, which opened on 30 August
1979, relied on the participation of anonymous individuals
who frequented the outdoor farmer's market held regularly on
Saturdays in the Grote Markt, in the centre of town. An advertisement placed in the newspaper *Nieuwsblad van het Noorden* on

a Friday announced, 'Je Eigen Telefoonnummer Op Een T shirt,
Grote Markt, Zaterdagen' ('Your own telephone number on
a T-shirt, Grote Markt, Saturdays'). The numbers '12 45 02',
representing a model number, appeared inside the accompanying
outline of a short-sleeved shirt. During the six weeks the work
lasted, as stated in the advertisement, T-shirts were available
for a modest price at a stand among the regular market vendors
of wares and produce. Designed by Asher, they were made of soft,
white cotton and possessed the same gently scooped neckline
whether turned front or back. Each shirt provided the surface on
which black numbers could be heat-transferred. These numbers,
aligned vertically two-by-two in Futura Bold typeface down
the centre of the garment, displayed the home telephone contact
of the person who purchased the shirt.

When individuals wearing the shirts emblazoned with their
phone numbers were spotted at the market, Asher's exhibition
was in full operation. Activated by each and every one of its
participants, the work rested in the hands of the random people
who came across — or were informed about — the Corps De Garde
concession, and who voluntarily bought and wore the shirts as
they perambulated the square and beyond. If the individuals
wearing the shirts directly contributed to the work's implemen-
tation, the passers-by more generally defined the viewing public.
People moving through the square could not help but notice the
garments, which presumably led them to question why fellow
strangers would display three vertically aligned couplets of
integers, possibly local telephone numbers printed on their
clothing. Although Asher deliberately relinquished authorial
control of his work in favour of the chance involvement of
willing participants (as opposed to hired individuals), he was
responsible for putting the elements of the work literally and
figuratively 'in place'. The work fanned out from the city centre
into the public domain, as those sporting the numbers on the

front or back of their shirts merged with the social fabric.
Having taken into account the all-pervasive ubiquity of public
display on clothing, Asher's shirts evidenced the dividing line
between adornment and advertising as much as the line between
public and private space. Simultaneously, he dispensed with
the need for museum walls and galleries, as the work, attached
to its sponsoring institutional auspices, radiated outward by the
movement of persons walking to and from the Saturday market.
Predicated on a low-cost transaction, the work also escaped
subjection to high-powered systems of economic exchange
incurred by art objects. Although outdoors, uncontained and
amorphous, the Groningen work possessed an affinity with
Kunsthalle Bern, 1992 to the degree that it, too, was constructed
on a model of circulation, if only the random circulation of
individuals in a town from a central point, as opposed to the
controlled circulation of hot water from wall valves to radiators
along a 'route' away from the boiler in the basement.

An international conference held from 9 to 11 October 1980
at the Université du Québec à Montréal (UQAM) marked the
occasion for a three-day installation by Asher at the invitation
of the contemporary art journal *Parachute*, under whose
auspices the conference 'Performance and Multidisciplinarity:
Postmodernism, a Colloquium on the Theory and Practice
of Contemporary Art' took place.[59] Although the colloquium
lasted only three days, films and performances were held at the
university throughout October and November. Asher, however,
chose to time his work to coincide with the conference, and took
inspiration from the school's main building, specifically its
tiered architectural configuration around a large, open, central
space resembling the layout of a shopping centre. Asher installed
his work on the communal video monitors that the university
routinely uses to dispense in-house information to students
and faculty. At half-hour intervals during the three-day period,

Asher presented a video loop of one of three shopping centres
in the Los Angeles area: Fox Hill Mall was shown on 9 October,
Old Town Mall on 10 October and Del Amo Fashion Square on 11
October. In addition to the video presentations, he placed three
black-and-white production stills (one from each of the videos)
side by side on the school's outdoor notice board at its rue Saint-
Denis entrance, where they remained for the duration of
Parachute's two-month programme of activities. From behind
the framed glass of the encased announcement board, Asher's
video stills gave the superficial impression, because of their
presentational context, of brokerage firm advertisements or
cinema production stills.

The three-day installation took full advantage of the sense
of immediacy created by the transmission of the video footage
taken at the three malls. On each of the three successive days,
the monitors displayed variations on the theme of consumerism,
as it played out specific reference to spaces constructed for
shopping. The shopping centres resonated with the architectural
character of UQAM's building, although they did not possess
the same degree of interior expanse apparent in the school's
premises, its several floors and its ample atrium with fountain
and trees. With its tiered levels surrounding an indoor core, Fox
Hill Mall most closely approximated the university's complex.
The most striking aspect of this particular mall was the degree
of blatant advertising marked by ubiquitously beckoning neon
signs and a barrage of commercial information. The entrances
of individual shops and businesses gave onto simulated outdoor
walkways, as if they were in the open air, all to disorienting
effect. The footage of Old Town Mall, not unlike that of Fox Hill,
emphasised the inherent artifice of shopping-centre architecture
in general, where, for example, a false outdoor street was enclosed
within the building. The accoutrements of the street, such as
lamp posts and bus benches, lined the ersatz avenue, while

architectural façades were designed in a number of pseudo-period styles. Visitors to this shopping centre could follow various pathways leading them to diversion and spending sprees.
In contrast, the architecture at Del Amo Fashion Square might be said to have consumed its consumers, captivating shoppers by means of reflective surfaces in which patrons could see themselves in the process of shopping. When looking up to mirrors in the ceiling, customers observed the reflections of themselves and others, while angles and disjunctions in the glass served to entrance, rather than to edify. As opposed to seventeenth-century Italian ceiling paintings, in which painted illusion ideationally passes as being real, the shiny surfaces of the shopping centre's ceiling deliberately distorted and distracted shoppers, seeking to waylay them rather than to inspire critical reflection or speculation.

The Montreal installation, carried out under the auspices of an art magazine, took place in a public arena associated with an educational facility instead of in an art museum or gallery. In this regard, the work could attend to contemporary culture's obsession with shopping — versus studying — and to the concomitant pursuit of tangible goods over the more elucidating pursuit of knowledge. By enlisting the technology then available for providing channels for political propaganda, Asher's work lent 'perspective' to its own and to viewers' contextual circumstance, transporting them to geographically distant yet analogous architectural surroundings. Footage on the monitors, spliced into the school's daily bulletins, reminded students and educators of their place in a society where sites of entertainment outnumber those of erudition, and where those of erudition are encroached upon by having to generate revenue rather than education, students are transformed into customers and knowledge into marketable goods. In the video images of the California shopping centres, students and faculty could observe,

in real time, the manipulation of architectural ruses for
encouraging acquisitive behaviour at the expense of inquisitive
thought, and draw comparisons to the changes taking place in
their own academic environment.

❀❀❀

Such attempts to expose artifice — of market economy, of
history and of social constructions, but also of art itself — have
characterised Asher's practice to date. Whether inside or outside
of the institution, his works have succeeded in reflecting on each
organisational situation, cutting through the false, the illusory
or the otherwise unperceived, to give material and ideational
form to transparency.[60]

Contemporaries of Michael Asher

Deriving the material properties of his work from the reality
of its contextual situation, Michael Asher imbues his art with
ever-new sets of terms that are based on the adoption of often
utilitarian and always pre-existing elements. With their ironic
tip of the hat to Minimal geometry and seriality, the Bern
radiators and heating pipes served to replace the conventions
of sculpture and filled the entirety of the exhibition space with
a dynamic working system. Asher has not been entirely alone
in his interaction with architecture, in his direct engagement
with the extant exhibition space, in his desire to reveal the
structures and conditions that comprise institutions and in his
questioning of the commodity nature of art. His oeuvre shares
ideas and methods with the artistic practice of contemporaries
who, residing on both sides of the Atlantic and emerging in
the second half of the 1960s, similarly rejected the material
and thematic autonomy of traditional painting and sculpture.
The works of Sol LeWitt, Mel Bochner, Blinky Palermo, Giovanni
Anselmo, Fred Sandback, Gordon Matta-Clark, Maria Nordman,
Marcel Broodthaers and Daniel Buren serve as cogent cases
in point for setting *Kunsthalle Bern, Bern, Switzerland, October
16—November 29, 1992* within its historical cognates in
connection with developments in installation art in the late
1960s. Participating in the genesis of new forms of art, these
artists, like Asher, discredited self-sufficient two- and three-
dimensionality in favour of works that self-referentially
acknowledge their attendant systems of support, whether this
be their perceived walls and spatial surrounds or, in addition,
their unperceivable socio-economic and cultural contexts.

Walls in Lieu of Canvases: The Exhibition Container

The concerns of LeWitt, Bochner and Palermo may be addressed
together with regard to their comparable turn from the creation
of framed depictions and solitary volumetric objects to works

associated with architecture. Having dispensed with canvas or pedestal, they defined the wall and the real space of the room as crucial to the realisation of their works. LeWitt, a major progenitor of installation art (and credited with the inaugural in-depth definition of the term 'Conceptual art'),[61] conceived his *Wall Drawings* (fig.40) subsequent to launching his Minimal structures. LeWitt's early *Wall Drawings* fuse drawing and architecture. Liberating drawn lines from subservience to a pictorial scheme, repeated linear elements promote themselves as self-fulfilling entities without submission to the purposes of outlining objects or of shading them by means of cross-hatching. In October 1968, LeWitt realised his first *Wall Drawing* for a group exhibition at Paula Cooper Gallery in New York. In what was at the time a radical move, he replaced the intermediary support of canvas or paper with the bare gallery wall. The next year, he carried his initial idea a step further, envisioning all the walls of the Dwan Gallery in New York as part of a single, all-encompassing work.[62]

Devising precise systems for covering walls with overall, non-hierarchical patterns of pencil, crayon or chalk lines, LeWitt documented his predetermined directives in the titles of his works. The *Wall Drawings* include, among many others, *Lines in Four Directions, in Four Colors, Superimposed* (1970), *Grid, Circles, Arcs from Four Sides and Four Corners* (1971) and *All Combinations of Arcs from Corners and Sides, Straight Lines, Not-Straight Lines and Broken Lines* (1973). The use of an advance plan was first articulated by LeWitt in his 'Paragraphs on Conceptual Art', published in *Artforum* in the summer of 1967. In order to excise random, extraneous or compositionally dominant shapes or images issuing purely from an artist's imagination rather than from rational necessity, LeWitt prescribed the adoption of self-imposed rules:

*To work with a plan that is pre-set is one way of avoiding
subjectivity. [...] The plan would design the work. [...]
The artist would select the basic form and rules that would
govern the solution of the problem. After that the fewer
decisions made in the course of completing the work the
better. This eliminates the arbitrary, the capricious, and
the subjective as much as possible. That is the reason for
using this method.*[63]

In LeWitt's early *Wall Drawings*, linear components following
a predetermined scheme hold sway over the entirety of one or
more walls to achieve the inextricable interlocking of figure
and ground. Whatever the scheme chosen by the artist, the *Wall
Drawings* speak for the paradigmatic shift in the late 1960s from
intermediary surface to the surface of the wall. Whereas the *Wall
Drawings*, however, remain within the surrounds of one room,
Asher's work in Bern took over the entirety of the Kunsthalle. Of
further note, the Kunsthalle work dispensed with the traditional
mediums for marking a surface — pencil or chalk — to utilise
steel pipes as lines.

Mel Bochner's *Measurement: Rooms*, part of his larger series
on measurement executed in 1968 and 1969, likewise bring the
walls of the exhibition space into direct purview. The rooms
evolved from the artist's 'desire for an art that did not add
to the furniture of the world',[64] and grew out of his previous
exploration of sculptural constructions via numerical systems
and photography. Bochner's earlier works (the ones he made
in 1965 and 1966) pointed to, but did not possess, the material
mass of traditional sculpture. In 1968 he further studied
correspondences between flat imagery recorded by a camera lens
and three-dimensional, material objects, which photography
claims to reproduce. For example, in the photograph *Actual Size
(Face)* made that year, a vertical line on the wall, parallel with

Bochner's profile, demarcates a span of 30 centimetres. Bochner
developed the film to the scale of his face, notionally adjusting
the supposed verisimilitude of mechanical reproduction to
fit the task of accurately registering objects in illusory space.

From such two-dimensional photographic works dealing with
issues of three-dimensionality, Bochner turned to a head-on
confrontation with spatial reality. In a *Measurement: Room*
(fig.37), black, half-inch-wide tape runs the length and height
of the exhibition walls, along baseboards, doorjambs and lintels.
Thin, black, Letraset numerals — adhered to the wall at strategic
breaks along the narrow, linear stretches of tape — indicate the
number of feet and inches calculated from point to point. 'When
I measure a room,' Bochner has said, 'it objectifies the emptiness
of the space. The measurements project a mental construct of the
space onto the space itself.'[65] On an abstract, ontological level, a
Measurement: Room divides an exhibition space into numerically
verifiable segments, although, on an observational level, the
room remains wholly intact as a space that can be entered and
used. Discarding the general conception of exhibition space as
unheeded container, the *Measurement: Rooms* function factually
and flatly, as well as volumetrically, on the plane of empirical
and epistemological experience. At the same time, much
as in Bern, the exhibition space is absorbed into the work's
representational content rather than merely serving as a neutral
backdrop for representation. Bern's hot-water pipes did exactly
this: they did not measure the rooms, like Bochner's lines,
but they did provide a visual lead for an appreciation of the
exhibition space as representational entity in and of itself as
Bochner, in parallel manner, aimed to convey.

Without knowledge of LeWitt's initial *Wall Drawing* in New
York, Blinky Palermo realised the first of his *Wandzeichnungen
und Wandmalerie* (*Wall Drawings and Paintings*) at Galerie Heiner

Friedrich in Munich in December 1968. He used reddish-brown
crayon to draw directly on the gallery walls a series of open,
outlined shapes based on the number '5'. Half a decade later,
in 1973, for a solo exhibition at the Kunstverein in Hamburg,
he made one of his final works, rendered on the wall by painting
the Kunstverein's free-standing, permanently positioned wall
partitions a deep red oxide. Presenting walls drenched in a single
colour, the exhibition, in its disavowal of traditional modes
of presentation, angered many of the city's residents, and the
exhibition was closed after the first week as a consequence of
these protests. Palermo's work in Hamburg was the culmination
of his diverse approaches to his *Wall Drawings and Paintings*,
almost all of which derived their pictorial form either from
the shapes of existing walls or architectural features or from
architectural elements transposed from outside sources. In 1971,
for his second exhibition at Galerie Heiner Friedrich, he painted
two of the gallery's facing walls in a reversed colour scheme:
one side was ochre rimmed by a narrow strip of white; the other
was white bordered in ochre. Thereby the walls — as well as the
doorways, which Palermo took care to include when outlining
each of the walls — stood out independently as shapes in and
of themselves. The year before, at the Kunsthalle Baden-Baden,
he had painted a blue line that followed the moulding just
below ceiling height to ring the entire exhibition space overhead
with an elegant, emphatic rectangle.[66] Also in 1970, for the
work *Fenster I (Window I)* at Kabinett für aktuelle Kunst in
Bremerhaven, Palermo copied to scale the structural outline
of the mullions of the museum's glass entryway on a wall of
the exhibition space. Taking a similar approach at the Konrad
Fischer Galerie in Düsseldorf, again in 1970, for *Treppenhaus
I (Stairwell I)*, he rendered the profile of another building's
staircase onto the gallery's wall, filling in the hard-edge zigzag
form with grey paint (fig.38). Serving as a prelude to his work
in Hamburg, Palermo's *Wall Drawings and Paintings* anticipated

the convergence of painting, sculpture and architecture within a unified whole in this later work. His Hamburg work, in this regard, shares much in common with Asher's Bern work, given its fusion of the linear, the sculptural and the architectural.

Redefining Sculpture through Architecture

LeWitt's *Wall Drawings*, Bochner's *Measurement: Rooms* and Palermo's *Wall Drawings and Paintings* interact with the walls of otherwise empty exhibition spaces to create rooms that are aesthetic totalities in and of themselves. In a similar vein, Anselmo and Sandback have made works that directly engage with the space that is occupied by viewers rather than seeking to create full-bodied material objects in the attempt to fill surrounding space as if it were an empty void.

Giovanni Anselmo's *Particolare* (fig.39) — originally shown at Galleria Sperone in Turin in 1972 — employs a projector to bring language into contact with the materiality of exhibition surfaces. The piece is a departure from his earlier three-dimensional works (often grouped with those by other Italian artists and the practices of Arte Povera), in which Anselmo sought to throw off the dead, inert weight of sculptural tradition. In one version of *Torsione* (*Torsion*, 1968), for example, the artist suspended an iron bar from a tightly twisted, fustian cloth. Hanging on the wall, it appears ready to unwind and spin, expressing a state of pent-up energy. In contrast, *Particolare* severs ties with volumetric materiality to enter into a dialogue with the spatial actuality of architectural confines. Projected on a variety of surfaces within a room, the word 'particolare' (Italian for detail, but also meaning peculiar, singular or strange) — rendered in small, lowercase type — animates and articulates the exhibition area. By means of multiple projectors, Anselmo often labels the floor, the wall and the ceiling along with other structural variables, such as a baseboard, a moulding,

a radiator or one of the projectors. Dispersed throughout
the space, the illuminated 'details' point to, and meld with,
the reality of their physical setting, while the work as a
whole presents itself as the ineluctable sum of its aggregate
architectural parts. Anselmo's linguistic intervention into the
exhibition space offers another example of the desire on the part
of Asher's contemporaries, beginning in the late 1960s and early
70s, to 'detail' or map a work's architectural support.

As early as 1966, when he was a student at Yale University School
of Art and Architecture, Fred Sandback began his exploration
of ways 'to make sculpture that didn't have an inside'.[67] By the
early 1970s, he was using coloured yarn to reconfigure sculpture
to intersect with what he termed 'pedestrian space' — an area
that may be thought of as 'literal, flat-footed and everyday'.[68] The
word 'pedestrian' possesses a double meaning, insofar as works
by Sandback occupy the same space through which viewers walk.
The thin, taut, coloured lines of string delineate open planes
in the middle of a room or in relation to a wall or corner. With
the sparest of material means, his work thus brings together
the normally separate disciplines of drawing, sculpture and
architecture to elide the two-dimensionality of painting and
the volumetric properties of sculpture within the actuality
of open space. Sandback's untitled yarn installations articulate
their spatial environment rather than depending on architectural surfaces (as do works by LeWitt, Bochner, Anselmo or
Palermo). Nonetheless, they may be included in the same breath
as works by Asher and his contemporaries in their mutual
quest to bring art in line with the observable reality of its
physical surrounds and architectural context. But, in distinct
differentiation from the methods of most of his contemporaries,
Asher did not draw, tape, project or paint on walls, or import
any secondary materials into the exhibition space. He simply
reoriented and redirected objects/materials that were already

functionally in use (if hidden, like the heating pipes behind the walls) within the Kunsthalle's galleries.[69] In this, he seems to follow Gordon Matta-Clark's words: 'Why hang things on a wall,' Matta-Clark queried, 'when the wall itself is so much more a challenging medium?'[70]

Architectural Site-Specificity

Matta-Clark's work — like that of Maria Nordman — parallels the thematic reach of Asher's investigations in the socio-economic sphere. Known for his dissection of buildings slated for demolition, Matta-Clark realised his first museum commission (and his last work) at the Museum of Contemporary Art in Chicago, in the newly acquired three-story townhouse prior to its renovation and transformation into gallery space. The piece, *Circus or The Caribbean Orange* (1978; fig.41), aimed to 'suggest ways of rethinking what is already there'.[71] Working diagonally from the basement to the roof, Matta-Clark used a chainsaw to make three large circular incisions, producing gigantic and dynamic arcs that spanned the entire width of the house. The massive cuts joined together living quarters that were once separate, as the chainsaw pierced through walls, floors and ceilings. At the same time that *Circus or The Caribbean Orange* created layered vistas into abandoned sites of domesticity, it also revealed formerly hidden, walled enclosures and strata indicative of social structures that can isolate, categorise or confine. Created from a formerly inhabited building, Matta-Clark's work functioned as a multifaceted, outsize, outdoor, enterable sculpture with its own indoor space. Although *Kunsthalle Bern, 1992* also dealt with, in Matta-Clark's words, 'what [was] already there', Asher's work remained enclosed within spatial confines. At the close of the exhibition, when the radiators were returned to their former locations, the exhibition space was restored to its previous condition without destruction of a building or damage to any part of one.

By the end of the 1960s Maria Nordman had received her Master
of Fine Arts degree from the University of California, Los
Angeles. She, like Asher, had begun her exploration of ways to
confront the observable world without resorting to intervening
forms of representation. Repudiating terminology such as
'viewer', 'spectator' or 'observer' in favour of phrases such as
'the unknown person' or 'any person arriving by chance', she
considers her art to be an activity that involves cooperation from
both informed and uninformed audiences alike.[72] As in *Untitled:
Newport*, one of her two major California museum installations
in 1973, Nordman adopted sunlight as her medium insofar
as the rays interact with existing architectural spaces as an
active force, and insofar as the built environment of architecture
belongs within the context of urban life. Sunlight, itself
invisible but making vision possible, changes constantly in
intensity, passes through or is reflected by glass, seeps through
crevices and permeates outdoor architectural cavities. Nordman
conceived *Untitled: Newport* for the Newport Harbor Art Museum,
where it could only be seen from an alley at the back of the
building. She requested that a relatively large, wedge-shape
cavity, painted white, be built in the museum's loading-dock
area. The space could not be entered from the museum, and to
see the work visitors had to exit and go to the alley at the back of
the building. Anyone walking to and from the Pacific Ocean also
passed by the structure, as it had been placed in relation to the
street, where, Nordman maintains, there are 'no preconceptions
about art'.[73] The artist calculated that the work, 'an event
initiated by the sun',[74] would be totally filled with light at
12.30 in the afternoon on 28 February 1973, the time and date
the exhibition opened. When this or a related work is realised,
full luminosity of the cavity — weather permitting — reaches
its peak at a slightly different time each day. At these culmina-
tions, the sun completely obliterates the angular lines of the
wedge-shape space, flooding it with a planar screen of intense

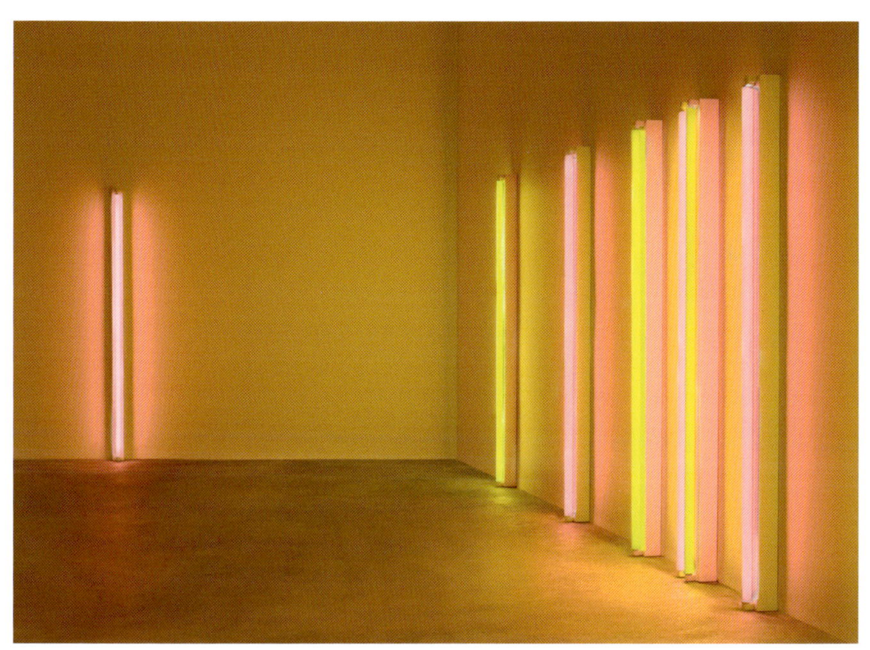

36. Dan Flavin,
alternating pink and 'gold', 1967,
pink and yellow fluorescent light,
244cm height, variable length
© Stephen Flavin/DACS, London;
ARS, New York
Courtesy David Zwirner, New York
Photograph: Cathy Carver

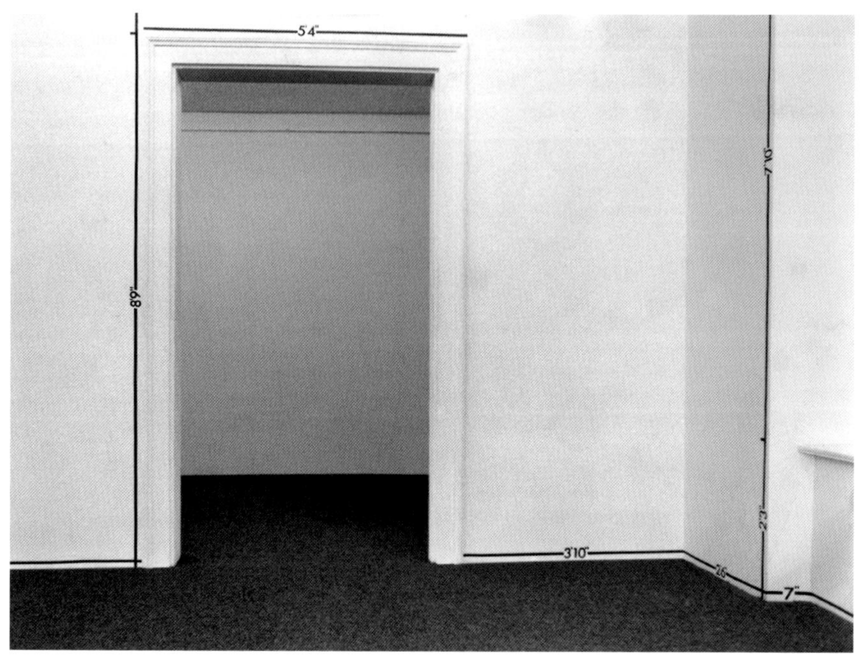

37. Mel Bochner,
Measurement: Room, 1969,
tape and Letraset on wall,
size determined by installation
Collection of the Museum of Modern Art,
New York

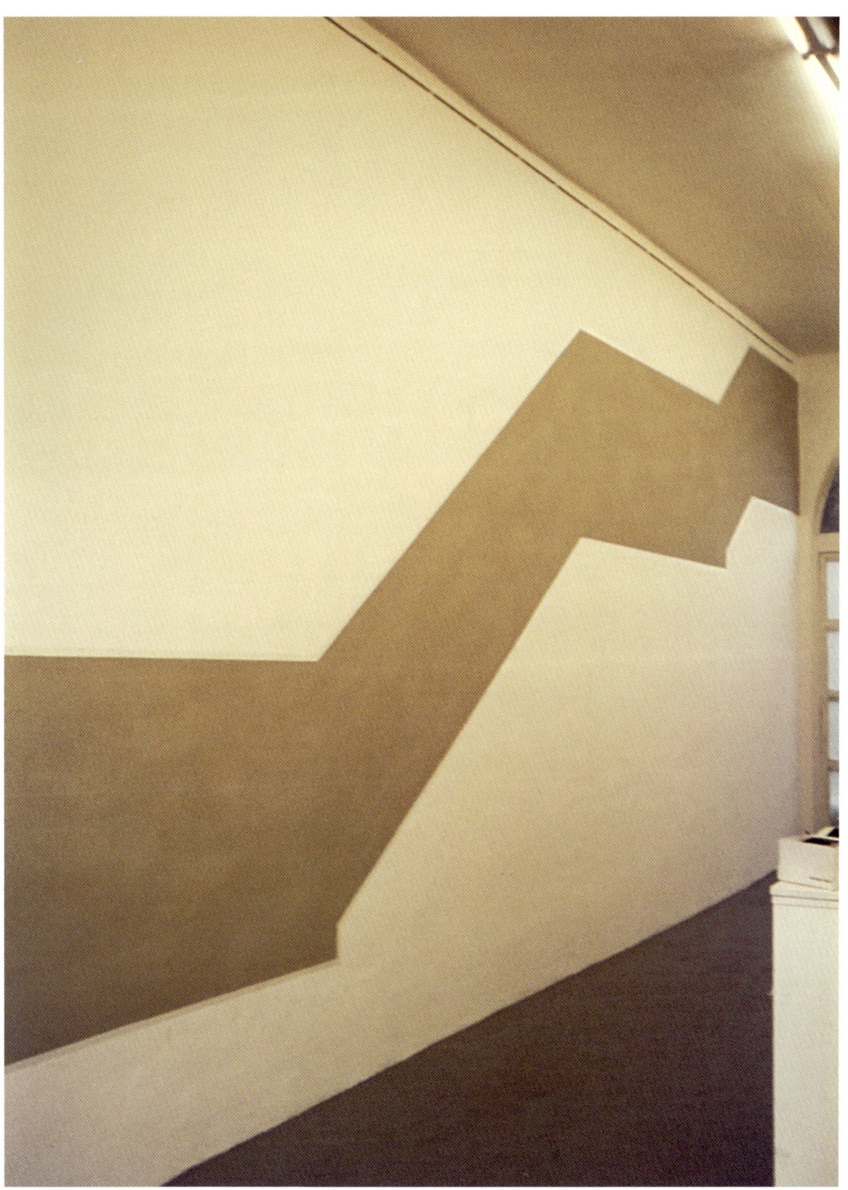

38. Blinky Palermo,
Treppenhaus I (Stairwell I), 1970,
paint on wall, 390 × 1,070cm,
installation view, Konrad Fischer Galerie,
Düsseldorf, 1970

© Blinky Palermo Estate
(Michael Heisterkamp)/DACS, 2012
Courtesy Konrad Fischer Galerie,
Düsseldorf
Photograph: Dorothee Fischer

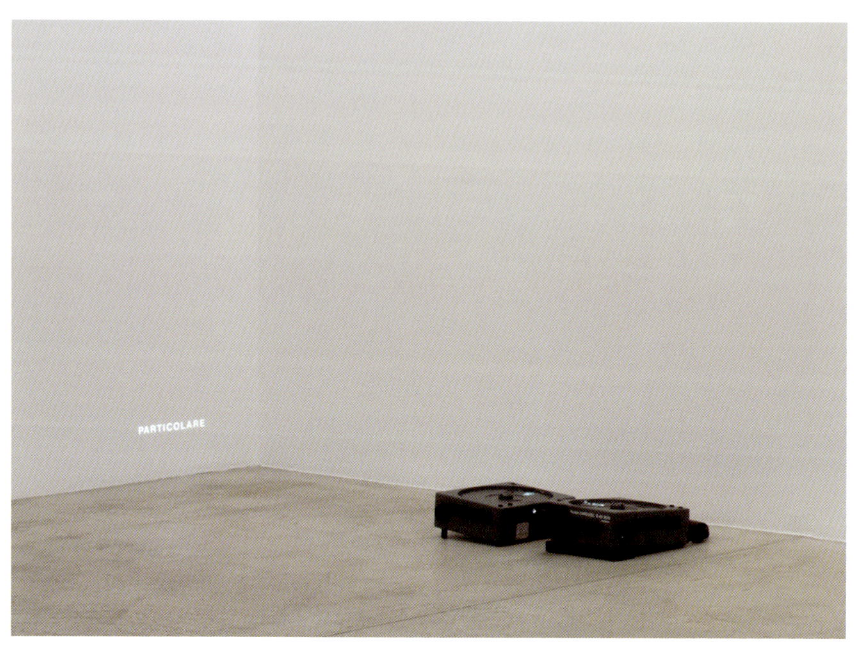

39. Giovanni Anselmo,
Particolare, 1972—2010,
two projectors, slides,
dimensions variable
Courtesy the artist and Marian Goodman
Gallery, New York/Paris

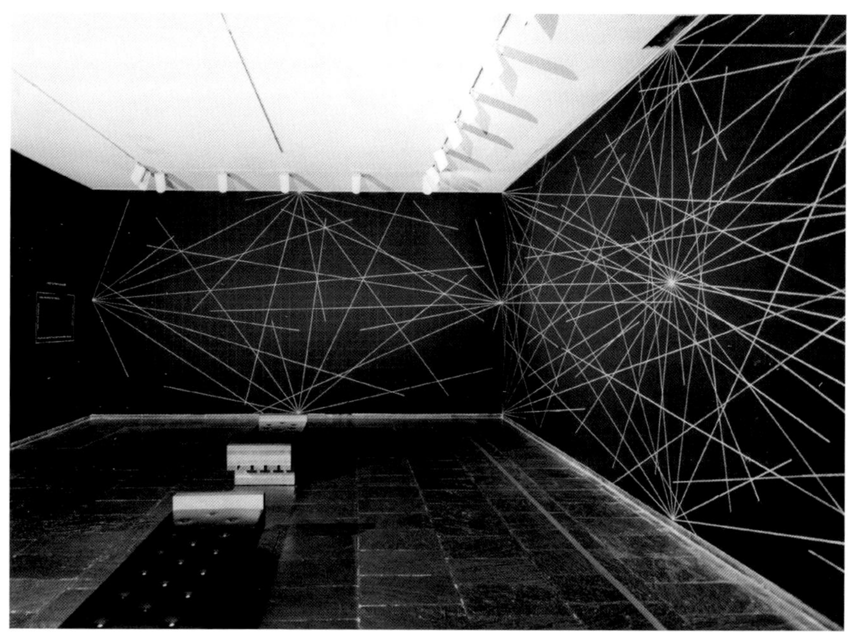

40. Sol LeWitt,
Wall Drawing #289: A six-inch (15 cm)
grid covering each of the four black walls.
White lines to points on the grids. 1st wall:
24 lines from the center; 2nd wall: 12 lines
from the midpoint of each of the sides; 3rd wall:
12 lines from each corner; 4th wall: 24 lines
from the center, 2 lines from the midpoint
of each of the sides, 12 lines from each corner
(The length of the lines and their placement
are determined by the drafter), 1976,
white crayon lines, black pencil grid,
black walls; installation view at the
Whitney Museum of American Art
Collection of the Whitney Museum
of American Art, New York, purchased
with funds from the Gilman Foundation
© Estate of Sol LeWitt 2012
Courtesy The Pace Gallery, New York

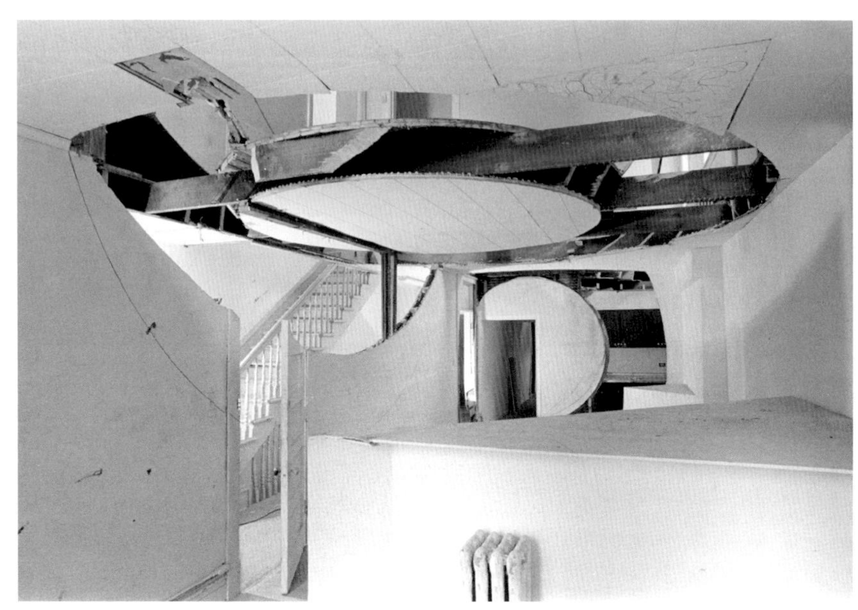

41. Gordon Matta-Clark,
Circus or The Caribbean Orange, 1978, Chicago
© The Estate of Gordon-Matta Clark /ARS
New York, DACS London
Courtesy The Estate of Gordon-Matta Clark
and David Zwirner, New York

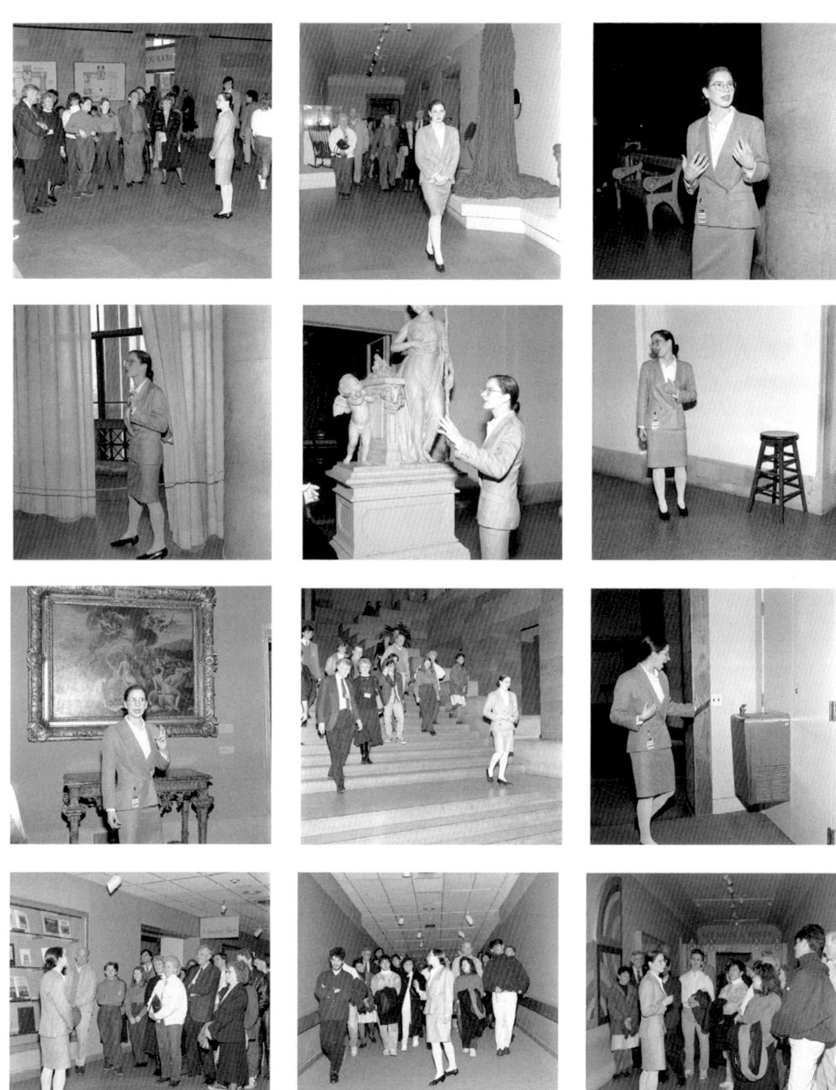

42. Andrea Fraser,
Museum Highlights: A Gallery Talk, 1989,
performance at the Philadelphia
Museum of Art,
Courtesy the artist
Photographs: Kelly & Massa Photography

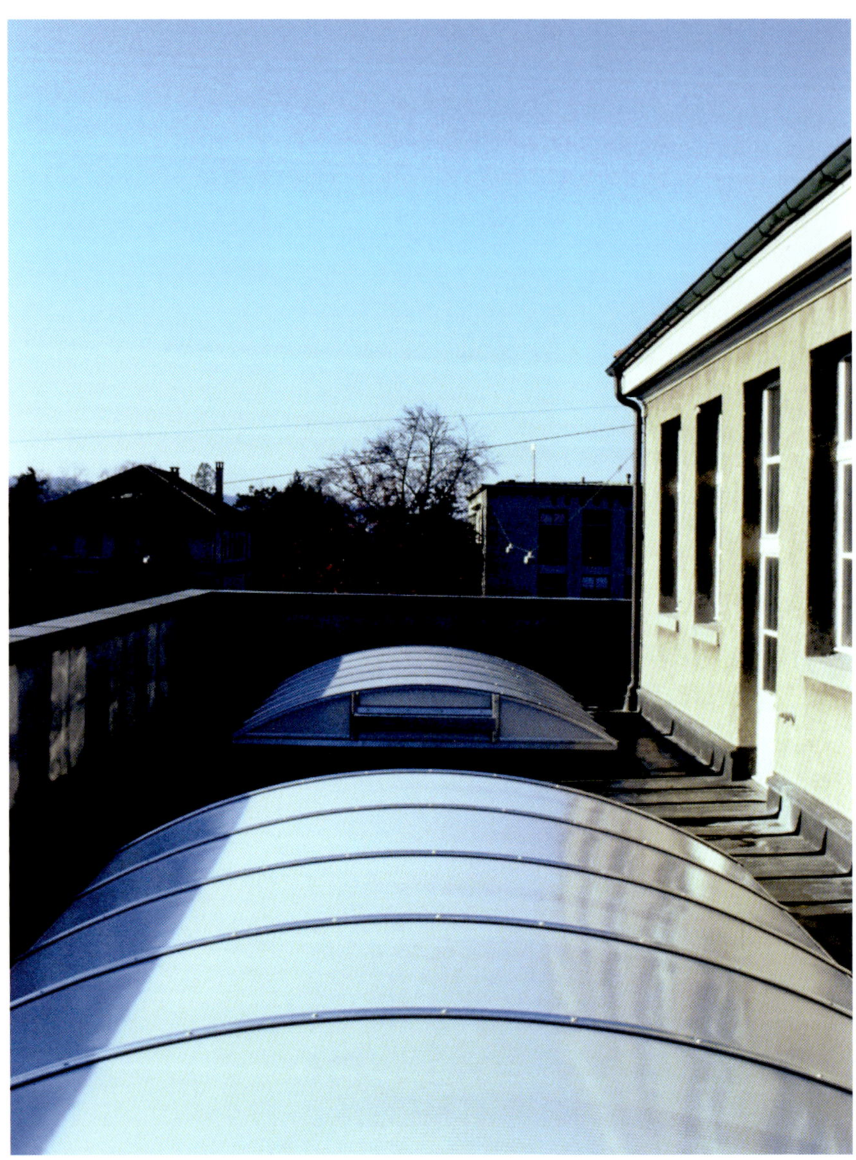

43. Maria Eichhorn,
Das Geld der Kunsthalle Bern
(*Money at Kunsthalle Bern*), 2001,
detail showing that leaking skylights
in the west and east halls have been replaced
with new ones; courtesy the artist
Photograph: Dominique Uldry

white light. The changing angle of the sun, in combination
with the weather conditions, produces variously shifting degrees
of luminosity at any one moment, and the structural articulation
of the cavity gradually becomes evident. Engaging both museum-
goers and passers-by, *Untitled: Newport* incorporates natural light
and atmospheric variation within an urban context. A work that
could be called 'sun-specific' more precisely than 'site-specific',
Untitled: Newport was constructed to create a pure perceptual
experience within the context of the street, disconnected
from the habits of museum presentation and reception. Such
disruption of habits was adopted by Asher in *Kunsthalle Bern,
1992*, when he reinstalled non-art fixtures already on-site and
identified them as the material basis of the work.

The Institutional and Cultural Context

Like Asher's aesthetic production, the works of Matta-Clark
and Nordman encompass social and economic content. Marcel
Broodthaers and Daniel Buren, in their mutual dedication to
pointedly raising questions concerning art in relation to its
cultural — and therefore institutional — context, highlight
a key interest of Asher's practice: the power of the museum
to bestow aesthetic value on whatever an artist has chosen to
present within its domain. This was pointedly exemplified by
Kunsthalle Bern, 1992's installation of its building's radiators
in lieu of individual 'art' objects, whether found or crafted by
the artist.

In 1972, Broodthaers created the work-turned-exhibition *Der
Adler vom Oligozän bis Heute* (*The Eagle from the Oligocene to the
Present*). Installed at the Kunsthalle Düsseldorf from 16 May to
9 July, the show addressed the commodity status of art and aimed
'to provoke critical thought about how art is represented in
public'.[75] Bearing the subtitle *Section des Figures* (*Figures Section*),
the exhibition was part of Broodthaers's larger project: the *Musée*

d'Art Moderne, Département des Aigles (*Museum of Modern Art,
Department of Eagles*, 1968—75). This fictional, itinerant
museum — for which Broodthaers served as self-appointed
director — organised a variety of exhibitions at different venues
over the course of its seven-year existence.

A seemingly exhaustive survey devoted to the subject of the eagle
from prehistoric to modern times, *Section des Figures* presented
a vast array of objects — 266 in all — that, for the most part,
the artist borrowed for the occasion from other museums and
collections throughout Europe.[76] The exhibition embraced
works from many different centuries in a wide range of media,
including paintings, sculpture, ceramics and textiles, as well
as functional objects (such as a 1910 Adler typewriter) and
remnants of popular culture (such as a cigar box, wine-bottle
labels and national emblems). Displayed on the wall or in
vitrines, each object was given equal play, whether a painting
of Ganymede by Peter Paul Rubens from the Museo del Prado
in Madrid; a page from a fifteenth-century codex borrowed
from a library in Zurich; a sixteenth-century tapestry from
the Kunsthistorisches Museum in Vienna; or a comic book
illustration. In the catalogue, written and designed by
Broodthaers himself, the works were organised alphabetically
by the city from which they had been procured, as opposed to
more customary categories such as artist, medium, subject matter
or date. In sum, the image of the eagle unified the extensive and
extremely varied array of assembled objects, all of which were
treated as if they possessed the same historical importance,
rarity and monetary worth.

Upon the dismantling of the Düsseldorf exhibition, the objects
could be neither sold nor, in all practicality, reassembled.
They could, however, be 're-collected' in memory as part of an
installation that blanketed art and non-art objects alike with

reference to a large cross section of images pertaining to the eagle that were held together by virtue of being within an art institution.[77] Within this context, Broodthaers replayed the museological processes of relocation and decontextualisation to which artworks in contemporary culture fall prey as commodities in the marketplace. Based on the same premise of the museum's institutional authority, *Kunsthalle Bern, 1992* inverted Broodthaers's stipulated denial that the art objects in his self-curated exhibition were not art. Asher, in reverse, took advantage of the fact that non-art objects are able to perform like art objects within an all-encompassing museological context in combination with an authorial behest.

In contrast to Broodthaers, who situated his installations within conventional exhibition areas, Daniel Buren has, since 1967, worked extensively outside of designated gallery spaces in a co-dependent relationship with the surfaces of existing architecture or with structures of quotidian urban life such as sailboats, buses and trains. He has used the phrase 'in situ' in reference to works that incorporate commercially obtained, prefabricated material printed with alternating white and single-colour bands of equal width (8.7 centimetres). By the mid-1960s, Buren had reduced the pictorial content of his paintings to vertical stripes with the intent of barring figuration and illusion from his canvases. A generic constant signifying painting, his signature stripes have appeared in hundreds of works worldwide, in which, again, art and non-art bond by means of this reductive sign/design. It may be applied to any surface to highlight any contextual situation both within and without museum or gallery walls. *Up and Down, In and Out, Step by Step: A Sculpture* (1977) inaugurated ensuing works for which he used flights of stairs. Buren conceived the installation for the group exhibition 'Europe in the Seventies: Aspects of Recent Art', organised by and presented at the Art Institute of

Chicago from 8 October to 17 November 1977. Ultimately purchased for the museum's permanent collection, the work comes into being when material, printed with white and colour vertical stripes, is cut and adhered to the risers of the Grand Staircase that connects the Michigan Avenue lobby with the second-floor galleries. For its first manifestation, Buren selected green and white stripes.[78] He also glued the striped material to the stairs leading to lower-level galleries and to the steps outside the front entrance, ushering visitors up to the 'hallowed halls' of art.

Up and Down combines painting, sculpture and architecture within a single aesthetic statement, while remaining in use as a means of ascent and descent by the public between different areas of the Institute. When its risers are striped, the staircase functions in its literal and metaphoric capacity to 'elevate' museum visitors as they proceed from the ground floor up to the Old Master galleries of painting, sculpture and decorative arts. And, in notable contrast to other works in the permanent collection — which are confined to pre-assigned rooms organised by systems of chronological or geographical classification and are subject to ongoing relocation — *Up and Down* physically and thematically interacts with the museum as an architectural edifice as well as an institutional and cultural totality. By virtue of its coinciding with the reality of the extant staircase, it singles out the entire sculptural form of the monumental flight of steps. At the same time, the work defines its own contextual setting within the visual grandeur of its spatial surroundings.

Buren's piece cannot be allocated to storage, borrowed or resold to another institution or private collection. As it appears/ disappears with each successive installation and dismantling, it will, in effect, keep in step with museological and art-historical changes while remaining an ever-present volumetric and

vibrant constant beneath visitors' feet as they ascend and
descend from one floor to another. Fixed in one location at the
focal point of the museum, and possibly changing in colour at
successive installations, *Up and Down* cannot be uprooted as a
(re)moveable object, remaining in place (and in situ) through
time at the architectural and institutional core of the museum.
In short, *Up and Down* cannot be physically extricated from
its architectural, institutional and culturally-defined setting.
It continues in its functional role when on view, as did the Bern
radiators, which were also contextually grounded in one place
by being attached to their respective pipes.

All these works contain an individual quest to bring art and
reality closer together in actual and ideational terms. This has
involved each artist in a search for strategies for establishing
an accord between an object and its visible spatial surrounds,
as well as, in some cases, between its invisible economic systems
of support. In one way or another, Asher's contemporaries have
similarly bound the physical reality of architecture and empty
space and the realities of the socio-economic system with
installations that do not remain intact when severed from their
sites. Works by LeWitt, Bochner, Anselmo, Sandback, Nordman
and, if only in theory, Broodthaers, may be reinstalled at other
times and venues. In contrast, those considered here by Palermo,
Matta-Clark and Buren assume full site-specific status, along
with Asher's work at the Kunsthalle Bern, by virtue of the
immutable material and thematic associations they established
with their contexts; in many instances, they survive only
through documentation and memory.

The Critique of the Object and the Object of Critique:
Michael Asher and his Influence

Two recent works by Michael Asher — a solo exhibition at
the Santa Monica Museum of Art (SMMOA) in 2008, and *No Title*
(2010), shown in the Whitney Museum of American Art's 2010
Biennial,[79] attest to the broad scope of a practice that, in its
basic terms, can be said to be founded on a critique of the discrete
materiality of traditional sculpture that does not attend to,
or reflect upon, the contextual conditions of its institutional
site. Although they appear to be poles apart visually and
experientially, these two works correspond conceptually not only
to each other but also to Asher's entire aesthetic output, and offer
fresh insight into the place *Kunsthalle Bern, Bern, Switzerland,
October 16—November 29, 1992* holds within his career.

For his exhibition in Santa Monica, fortuitously coinciding with
SMMOA's twentieth anniversary, Asher reconstructed the wall
studs of the exhibitions for which temporary partitions had been
built — most of which were made of metal, and some of wood.
All exhibitions after 1998, the year the museum moved to their
Bergamot Station location, were included.[80] (In about eleven
instances, the museum did not find the use of wall partitions
necessary.)[81] The individual floor plans for each show were hung
as points of reference on the wall of a small side room. In the
large main gallery, an intersecting, skeletal profusion of all the
once-existing wall studs (ghosts brought back in the flesh, one
might say) minus drywall filled the entire room and offered the
visual excitement of a transparent maze (fig.36). Not unlike the
dynamic movement of the heating pipes coursing throughout the
Kunsthalle Bern, the wall studs, paralleling and overlapping one
another in SMMOA's skylit rectangular space, created a dazzling
effect. An enterable, all-encompassing environment, described
by one critic as 'a walk-in puzzle',[82] Asher's Santa Monica work
enmeshed viewers within a labyrinth constructed on the basis of

once-extant partitions that had changed their configurations over the museum's ten-year history at its current location. To view the work, the visitors navigated to and from the gallery's entryway to the museum's back-door exit. The process entailed stepping in between the repetition of equally spaced vertical bars and over the great number of baseboard stud supports underfoot. Overhead, one could observe the multitude of interconnecting crossbars.

The exhibition, in one respect, was about openness on a number of levels: the literal openness of the studs left bare, which created vistas in multiple directions; the idea of opening up the museum's installation history to retrospective study; and the opening of the aesthetic object to examination in tandem with the opening of the work's venue to investigatory review. With its visual articulation of the structural underpinnings of bygone and impenetrable wall partitions, the installation physically contained its viewers within its confines, without restraining them. Promoting movement, it allowed visitors to circulate amid the physical structure formed by the studs, and counteracted the mandate to keep the sculpture's viewer at arm's length.

In marked contrast to this installation, *No Title*, Asher's work for the Whitney Biennial, did not alter any area of the museum or include a take-away item. He neither added nor subtracted any three-dimensional components — as he had done in Bern — to or from the work or the museum, but nonetheless affected the dynamics of the institution itself. Asher's project was communicated on standard wall labels mounted near the elevators on the three floors of the biennial. Also, as a part of the work he adhered large, black letters — about twenty-centimetres high — to the glass of the window facing Madison Avenue, reading 'Open All Day and Nite'. The typeface he chose, called Superstudio and suggested by the Whitney's graphic designer, could be read quickly and easily from the street, especially as

'all' and 'and' were written on a 45-degree angle. The official
press release, echoing the information on the wall labels, stated:

> *Michael Asher's proposal for the Whitney Biennial is to have
> the exhibition open continuously to the public twenty-four
> hours a day for one week (Monday, May 24 through Sunday,
> May 30).*
> *Note: The duration of this work has been shortened from
> the artist's original proposal. Due to budgetary and human
> resources limitations, the Museum is unable to remain
> open to the public twenty-four hours a day for one week.
> As a result, this work has been shortened from seven days
> to three days (Wednesday, May 26 at 12:00 am through
> Friday, May 28 at 11:59 pm).*

The proposal to make the museum open to the public for several
days on a 24-hour basis lifted — and drew attention to — the
restrictions on museum access necessitated by a paucity of
financial resources, which, ironically, go hand-in-hand with
the museum as a facility for educational 'enrichment'. In this,
the work recalled the exhibition practice of Group Material,
and their insistence on maintaining late opening hours in order
to allow people to attend an exhibition after work, a gesture
that identified working-class locals as their target audience.[83]
In its dependence on both public and private funding, the art
institution may be seen as a microcosm for the way in which
cultural — and mind-expanding — activity requires myriad
infusions of monetary sustenance derived from the highly
complex nexus of social and economic interactions and transactions contributing to its survival. *No Title* addressed the notion
of openness with reference to the museum as a physical plant
that rests not solely on concrete blocks, but on the intangible
economic systems making its operation viable. By virtue of his
authorial position, Asher effectively absorbed the entire museum

as a structure of edification into an artwork that subsumed
within its own parameters all other works on view, both
permanent and temporary, as well as all viewers entering
and exiting its premises during the specified three-day period.
Those visiting the institution at normal opening hours could
imagine the free flow of people, singly or in clusters, who
were at liberty to come and go through the Whitney's doors
at whatever hour suited them. In the process of imagining
No Title on site, visitors and non-visitors alike could ponder
connections between the institution of art, generally speaking,
and the particular institutions wherein objects of aesthetic
production are contextualised thematically, geographically
or chronologically, while indirectly being invested with
economic value through institutional validation and valorisa-
tion. Like *Kunsthalle Bern, 1992*, Asher's Whitney Biennial
work encompassed the totality of the museum's exhibition
area but, contrastingly, left it physically intact. Lodged within
the museum, *No Title* simply opened the institutional doors
to interrogative contemplation.

Asher's involvement with museological practices in his own
art has resonated with a subsequent generation of younger artists,
including Fred Wilson, Maria Eichhorn and Andrea Fraser, to
name only a few whose work is often addressed under the phrase
'institutional critique'.[84] By the time he represented the United
States at the Venice Biennale in 2003, Wilson had become well-
known for his artist-as-curator installations. His seminal 1992
exhibition 'Mining the Museum' was initiated at the invitation
of the Contemporary Museum in Baltimore, in collaboration
with the Maryland Historical Society, where it took place.
Utilising the entire third floor, Wilson reinstalled art and
artefacts from the society's collection in order to investigate
multi-pronged racial stereotyping. For example, he made a
pointed analogy between duck hunting and the capturing of

runaway slaves in the South of the United States when he aligned the long barrel of a gun for shooting game birds with a wood doll of an African American male.[85]

Andrea Fraser has articulated her own involvement in the evolution of the phrase 'institutional critique'.[86] A prolific writer and 'self-described autodidact',[87] she began her career with live performances. Two performances recorded on video evidence how she has examined facets and foibles of museums in order to feature aspects of institutional functioning. In *Museum Highlights: A Gallery Talk* (1989; fig.42), she takes on the persona of a fictional museum docent named Jane Castleton as she leads a group through the Philadelphia Museum of Art. In an extroverted and expansive-yet-deadpan manner, she gestures in the direction of objects, such as a drinking fountain, or speaks of areas of the museum, such as the cafeteria, in the absurdly superlative, if vacuous, language sometimes heard on guided tours.[88] In *Little Frank and His Carp* (2001), the artist is listening to the recorded audio guide available at the Guggenheim Museum in Bilbao, housed in the flamboyant building designed by architect Frank Gehry. As the voice on the recording describes the museum's architecture, the artist, in person, responds to the text as if it were a narration about an 'erotic encounter' with the building's undulating surfaces and curves. Although far from the stolid relationship with architecture or erasure of authorial presence found in *Kunsthalle Bern, 1992*, Fraser's performed work in Bilbao owes a debt to the oeuvre of Asher. Fraser has spelt out the high esteem in which she holds him, stating in a recent monographic article that Asher's work 'had a profound influence on my development as an artist'.[89]

In a different vein, without the artist's own presence, Maria Eichhorn's practice is concerned with questions about institutional critique in relation to cultural activity in capitalist society. Her 2001 exhibition *Das Geld der Kunsthalle Bern* (*Money at Kunsthalle Bern*), installed nearly a decade after Asher's show at the same venue, channels the making of art into a kind of social give-and-take, eschewing the creation of material objects whose value is economically as well as aesthetically based. In her words,

> *The value of money mirrors the relationships of society such as unemployment, inflation and deflation. If money is not turned into capital, its value declines. Turning money into commodities that appreciate in value affirms the status quo of capitalism.*[90]

For *Money at Kunsthalle Bern*, Eichhorn funded necessary repairs to the interior and exterior of the museum's building, from leaking skylights to worn-out plumbing. Museum staff members led exhibition visitors to the areas under repair, which included behind-the-scenes spaces for storage and a trip up a ladder to the skylight with a view overlooking the city (fig.43).[91] Additionally, a catalogue documented the history of Kunsthalle Bern's funding methods since the time of its founding, and Eichhorn issued an unlimited edition of share certificates for expansion of the museum's coffers. Most interestingly, Eichhorn's exhibition, like Asher's earlier, did not contain objects brought in from outside of the building, but pertained directly to the building itself. What distinguished the two exhibitions was the degree of physicality expressed. Whereas Asher's radiators and heating pipes assumed a sculptural — albeit highly untraditional — presence, Eichhorn's renovations merged with 'business as usual', or at least with business as it should be carried out when an institution's facility is in need. Following in Asher's foot- steps, Eichhorn based her aesthetic innovation on renovation. In 2001, she carried the ideas Asher played out in 1992 to a more overtly manifested economic plane. Following his paradigmatic example of subverting the creation of economically buoyed,

isolated objects, she replaced medium-based representation with
the actuality of a monetary transaction, along with the literal
enumeration of financial facts in the accompanying catalogue.

The impulse to resist the creation of singular material objects by
artists responding to precedents set by Asher and his generation
has necessarily assumed diverse aesthetic forms, as suggested
by the works of Wilson, Fraser and Eichhorn. Taking their cue
from their immediate predecessors, all three have dispensed
with the production of discrete objects by turning to installation
art or time-based mediums and performance. Indebted to the
groundwork laid by Asher, works by these and other artists have
furthered the preceding generation's endeavours by treating the
museum as a platform for addressing socio-economic questions,
by means of overt commentary through the unorthodox inclusion
and juxtaposition of objects within mock-curatorial installations, the outright parody of institutionalized relations with
the public or the inversion of habitual display processes within
institutional parameters. Asher's work at the Kunsthalle Bern
dramatically illustrated the weaving together of object and
museum into a seamless whole that alluded to the economic forces
accompanying art's possession and presentation. By pushing the
former limits of the material, visible art object toward ever-
greater transparency, Asher has succeeded throughout his career
in maintaining the critical place for aesthetic endeavour
within the social shape — a place where art might assert its
own self-analytic, ideational reality in the face of illusion.
To such an end, Asher has pried open the door to an awareness of
institutional practices by linking them inextricably with his
aesthetic practice. In his continuation of the modernist quest for
self-reflectivity, he has redirected art beyond the self-sufficiency
of a painting or a sculpture, and has done this by bringing to light
the invisible structures and driving forces that underlie the
supposed neutrality of art-exhibition spaces.

1
Asher pointed out that previous exhibiting artists often found these 'sarcophagi'
to be an intrusion, whereas, for him, they sparked the work's conception.
Conversation with the author, 31 January 2012.

2
The heating system at Kunsthalle Bern is a hot-water closed system, processed by
a circulating pump, with a gas boiler in the building's cellars. The radiators and
original pipe work are made of cast iron. The pipes used for the 1992 installation
were steel, made by Mannesmann. The architect who planned the installation was
Andreas Fuhrer from Bern, and the company that installed everything was Andrini
AG Heizungen, also from Bern. Approximately 850 metres of pipe were ordered.
Emails from Kunsthalle Bern staff, 24 April and 22 May 2012.

3
For a description, see Dieter Schwarz, 'Displacement', in Ulrich Loock (ed.),
Michael Asher, 16 October — 29 November 1992 (exh. cat.), Bern: Kunsthalle Bern,
1995, p.79ff.

4
Conversation with the artist, 10 April 2012.

5
Although each radiator to this day possesses its own regulator, there is only one
thermostat controlling the amount of heat for the building as a whole. This is
situated on the north elevation. Email from Kunsthalle Bern staff, 22 May 2012.

6
The titles of Asher's works include the name of the exhibition venue, its geographical
location and the exhibition's dates (in this order).

7
U. Loock, 'Michael Asher in Bern', in *ibid.*, p.9.

8
Birgit Pelzer, 'Entropy', in *ibid.*, p.69.

9
Ibid., p.75.

10
D. Schwarz, 'Displacement', *op. cit.*, p.82.

11
Michael Asher has stated that it took him quite some years to come up with
a solution for this work and that he had never thought of radiators or pipes in
any other connection before it. Conversation with the author, 27 May 2012. Asher
also designed the exhibition poster using the colours of the city's trams.

12
Asher chose the wall colour for the texts in accordance with the university's school
colour (and the name of its newspaper, *The Maroon*).

13
For an in-depth historical account of the Arts and Crafts movement in Britain and
the United States, see Eileen Boris, *Art and Labor: Ruskin, Morris, and the Craftsman
Ideal in America*, Philadelphia: Temple University Press, 1986.

14
For further information on the writings of the professors, see Anne Rorimer,
'Michael Asher: His Work at the Renaissance Society, Chicago', *Afterall*, issue 1,
Autumn/Winter 2000, pp.18—26. See also B. Pelzer, 'The Functions of Reference',
in Suzanne Ghez (ed.), *Michael Asher* (exh. cat.), Chicago: Renaissance Society,
University of Chicago, 1990, which includes illustrations of the text on the
nine panels.

15
The handout was held in a plastic box in one of the four alcoves in the corners of
the room, and was free for visitors to take.

16
The exhibition began on 22 May 1991 and lasted until all the cast-iron pieces were
distributed (so that there is no clear end date for this exhibition). Email from the
artist, 27 May 2012.

17
See M. Asher, 'Introduction', in *Michael Asher* (exh. cat.), Villeurbanne: Le Nouveau
Musée, 1991, p.8.

18
The full text on the cast-iron pieces includes additional language. One side reads:
'Cet objet a été coulé à partir de la fonte des anciennes chaudières du Nouveau
Musée à Villeurbanne au début de sa rénovation en Février 1991. Il est destiné à être
distribué gratuitement aux residents à revenue modestes dont le droit au logement
est menacé.' ('This object has been poured from melting the old boilers of the New
Museum in Villeurbanne at the beginning of its renovation in February 1991.
It is intended to be distributed free of charge to residents of modest income whose
right to housing is threatened.') On the other side the text reads: 'Se loger est un
droit! N'acceptez pas l'expulsion ou la discrimination. Renseignez vous auprès de:
Action Lyonnaise pour L'insertion Social par le Logement: 78 39 26 38; Association
Villeurbannaise pour le droit au logement: 78 94 95 61.' ('Housing is a right!
Do not accept eviction or discrimination. Please inquire with: Action Lyonnaise
pour L'insertion Social par le Logement: 78 39 26 38; Association Villeurbannaise
pour le droit au logement: 78 94 95 61.')

19
For further discussion, see Frederik Leen, 'Asher's Model of Mimetic Reality/
Rational Mimesis' (trans. Anne Marie Bony), in *Michael Asher* (exh. cat.),
Villeurbanne: Le Nouveau Musée, 1991, pp.12—56.

20
For more information, see Abigail Solomon-Godeau, 'Anywhere But Here: Michael
Asher's Consortium Installation' and Frederik Leen, 'The Logistics of Ambulatory
Behaviour', in Xavier Douroux, Franck Gautherot and Pascal Pique (ed.), *Michael
Asher: Le Consortium Dijon* (exh. cat.), Dijon: Le Consortium, 1991.

21
See B. Pelzer, 'L'Instance de Detail', in Jean-Michel Foray (ed.), *Michael Asher: Centre Georges Pompidou, Musée National d'Art Moderne, Galeries Contemporaines* (exh. cat.), Paris: Centre Georges Pompidou, 1991, pp.24—37.

22
Conversation with the artist, June 1991.

23
At Asher's request, the museum waived the entrance fee to his exhibition.

24
For a description and detailed analysis of this work, see B. Pelzer, 'Byways of History' (trans. Simon Pleasance), in *Michael Asher* (exh. cat.), Brussels: Société des Expositions du Palais des Beaux-Arts de Bruxelles, 1995, pp.29—38.

25
Ibid., p.32.

26
Ibid., p.35.

27
M. Asher quoted in Ann Goldstein, 'Artists in the Exhibition: Michael Asher', in A. Goldstein and Lisa Gabrielle Mark (ed.), *A Minimal Future? Art as Object: 1958—1968* (exh. cat.), Los Angeles, Cambridge, MA and London: Museum of Contemporary Art and The MIT Press, 2004, p.152.

28
Flavin quoted in Evelyn Weiss, Dieter Ronte and Manfred Schneckenburger (ed.), *Dan Flavin: Drei Installationen in floureszierendem Licht* (exh. cat.), Cologne: Kunsthalle Köln, 1973, p.87.

29
Ibid., p.84.

30
M. Asher, 'April 11—May 3, 1969, *18' 6" × 11' 2 1/2" × 47' × 11' 3/16" × 29' 8 1/2" × 31' 9 3/16"*, San Francisco Art Institute, San Francisco, California', in M. Asher and Benjamin H.D. Buchloh, *Writings 1973—1983 on Works 1969—1979*, Halifax and Los Angeles: The Press of the Nova Scotia College of Art and Design and Museum of Contemporary Art, 1983, p.1.

31
Ibid., p.5.

32
Similarly, in the Newport Harbor installation, Asher documented that 'a planar body of air was located just inside the main passageway to the inner gallery of the museum'. *Ibid.*, p.6.

33
Ibid., p.89.

34
M. Asher and B.H.D. Buchloh, 'September 21—October 12, 1974, Claire Copley
Gallery, Inc., Los Angeles, California', *Writings 1973—1983 on Works 1969—1979*,
op. cit., p.100.

35
In conversation with the author on 25 May, 2012, Claire Copley remembered
feeling 'like a gold fish in a bowl'. Her gallery opened in September 1973 (and closed
in 1978). Asher's display followed exhibitions by William Wegman, Ger van Elk,
William Leavitt, Lyn Horton, Allen Ruppersberg, Harriet Korman and Michael
Train. Because of the lack of venues for local critical writing at the time, Copley
took it upon herself to respond to annoyed and fascinated visitors alike who
wanted an explanation of the work, and who typically asked her 'where's the show?'
See also Kirsi Peltomäki, *Situation Aesthetics: The Work of Michael Asher*, Cambridge,
MA and London: The MIT Press, 2010, pp.76—81, for citations from *Artforum* and
Art International reviews of the exhibition as well as from correspondence from
Copley to Asher.

36
Asher's installation took place in advance of the museum's expansion in 2003.

37
M. Asher, 'August 3—August 29, 1977, Stedelijk Van Abbemuseum Eindhoven,
Netherlands', in M. Asher and B.H.D. Buchloh, *Writings 1973—1983 on Works
1969—1979, op. cit.*, p.178.

38
Ibid.

39
Typed sheet distributed to the public by the Museum of Contemporary Art. At the
end of the handout Asher states: 'This work belongs to the museum's permanent
collection. It is intended to be repeated each year for approximately two months,
or the length of a temporary exhibition.' See Appendix B of B.H.D. Buchloh,
'Michael Asher and the Conclusion of Modernist Sculpture', *Neo-avantgarde
and Cultural Industry — Essays on European and American Art from 1955 to 1975*,
Cambridge, MA and London: The MIT Press, 2003, p.32.

40
Ibid.

41
While Asher's first installation of the Bergman Gallery piece was on view,
the Museum of Contemporary Art also mounted the Sol LeWitt retrospective
organised by MoMA in 1978. LeWitt's *Lines from the Center of the Wall, Four Corners,
and Four Sides to Points on a Grid* (1976) was drawn in white chalk on black in
the available wall space between the aluminium panels.

42
Five months prior to the actual installation of the work, the Museum of
Contemporary Art bought the work for its permanent collection. According to
Asher's instructions, specified in the acquisition contract, the work would stop
being part of the collection as soon as the structure of the building was altered.
At the time plans for the 1996 move were already being discussed. See B.H.D.
Buchloh, 'Michael Asher and the Conclusion of Modernist Sculpture', *op. cit.*, p.28.

43
See Laslo Glozer (ed.), *Westkunst: Zeitgenössiche Kunst seit 1939* (exh. cat.), Cologne:
DuMont Buchverlag, 1981.

44
See K. Peltomäki, *Situation Aesthetics: The Work of Michael Asher*, *op. cit.*, pp.155—59

45
Text given to the author by the artist.

46
Kasper König remembers that when the funds for 'Westkunst' dwindled, 'Heute'
was made possible by the support of the participating dealers. Of the galleries
invited to participate a number were not physically present and therefore did
not lend chairs. Email to the author 30 May 2012. The participating dealers
who did not lend chairs were Galerie Krinzinger, Innsbruck; Metro Pictures,
New York; Sperone Gallery, Rome; Galerie Helen van der Meij, Amsterdam;
Bruno Bischofberger, Zurich; and Holly Solomon Gallery, New York.

47
For an illustration of Asher's proposal, see Susan Wyatt and Valerie Smith (ed.),
Michael Asher/James Coleman (exh. cat.), New York: Artists Space, 1988, p.19.
For further details about this work and the 'dynamic between the two physical
models of alternative space [...] — raw space as antidote to the traditional
gallery space and the white cube as duplication of it', see Martin Beck, 'Alternate:
Space', in Julie Ault (ed.), *Alternative Art: New York, 1965—1985*, New York
and Minneapolis: The Drawing Center and University of Minnesota Press, 2002,
pp.268—74. According to Beck, Asher extended the partitions of the renovation
under the direction of Ross Anderson 44 inches (111 centimetres) in a space that
was 16 feet high (4.8 metres).

48
Asher stipulated that his unpainted wall extensions could be patched and painted
to seamlessly match the white of the partitions after the closure of the exhibition
and the dismantling of his work, if Artists Space so chose. See *ibid.*, pp.273—74.
According to Beck, Artists Space took advantage of this option, thereby signalling
'the paradigmatic shift that occurred during the 1980s and that transformed the
conception of alternative space' from its 1970s accommodation to rawness to its
subsequent incorporation of pristine white surfaces on which to hang works by
emerging artists.

49
The exhibition took place from 18 November 1983 to 18 July 1985.

50
The exhibition took place from 9 June to 12 August 1979, and included work by, among others, Robert Barry, Dan Graham, Agnes Martin, Maria Nordman, Allen Ruppersberg and Lawrence Weiner.

51
Editors' note: Typed sheet distributed to the public by the Art Institute of Chicago. See Appendix A of B.H.D. Buchloh, 'Michael Asher and the Conclusion of Modernist Sculpture', *op. cit.*, pp.31—32.

52
Asher revisited this work in 2005, at which time several factors had changed. The Art Institute had reinstalled and changed the location of its eighteenth-century European painting, sculpture and decorative art rooms, and *George Washington* had been restored to its original bronze colour and sheen. See Whitney Moeller, '"George Washington" at the Art Institute of Chicago, 1916—2006' and A. Rorimer, 'focus: Michael Asher', in James Rondeau (ed.), *Michael Asher: George Washington at the Art Institute of Chicago, 1979 and 2005*, Chicago, New Haven and London: Art Institute of Chicago and Yale University Press, 2006, pp.14—27 and 28—33.

53
See Jennifer King, 'Perpetually Out of Place: Michael Asher and Jean-Antoine Houdon at the Art Institute of Chicago', *October*, vol.120, Spring 2007, pp.71—86.

54
12 June—1 August 1982, with work by 37 artists.

55
The designated half-hour-a-day time period was a practical matter. The viewers were mainly enlisted from members of the museum's staff, were regularly available at lunch hour and were paid a token fee for their services. For further discussion of this work, see K. Peltomäki, *Situation Aesthetics: The Work of Michael Asher*, *op. cit.*, p.88ff.

56
For an illustration of the poster and description of the work, titled in the catalogue *Sign in the Park*, see Stephanie Barron (ed.), *The Museum as Site: Sixteen Projects* (exh. cat.), Los Angeles: Los Angeles County Museum of Art, 1981, p.35.

57
The exhibition, curated by Kasper König, was open from 3 July to 13 November. The other participants were Carl Andre, Joseph Beuys, Donald Judd, Richard Long, Walter De Maria, Bruce Nauman, Claes Oldenburg, Ulrich Rückriem and Richard Serra.

58
Asher has participated in the 1987, 1997 and 2007 iterations, also curated by König and different collaborators, using a trailer of the same design each time. Over the forty-year period, the exhibition has, following Asher's precedent-setting work, taken place in relation to the public spaces throughout the city rather than closer to the museum. Asher's revival of this work once a decade, furthermore, provides a record of urban change in and around Münster, since not all of the original locations

— reused whenever possible — have remained with the passage of time. For
correspondence between Asher and Kasper König, see J. King (ed.), '"Skulptur
Projekte in Münster": Excerpts from Correspondence 1976—1997', *October*, vol.120,
Spring 2007, pp.87—105.

59
For documentation of the lectures, performances, films and installations,
see Chantal Pontbriand (ed.), *Performance, Text(e)s, and Documents*, Montreal:
Parachute, 1981.

60
Asher's Montreal work bears comparison with video works by Dan Graham from
the late 1970s. For documentation of individual works by Graham, see B.H.D.
Buchloh (ed.), *Dan Graham: Video-Architecture-Television: Writings on Video and Video
Works 1970—1978*, Halifax and New York: The Press of the Nova Scotia College
of Art and Design and New York University Press, 1979; this volume includes a text
by Asher: 'Excerpts of a description from Notebook 1/11/76 describing the first
run through a television broadcast delivered 1/18/76 as a work for the groupshow
"Via Los Angeles" at Portland Center for the Visual Arts, Portland (Oregon)
1/9/76—2/8/76' (p.56).

61
LeWitt's 'Paragraphs on Conceptual Art' (1967) and 'Sentences on Conceptual Art'
(1969) not only synthesised principles underlying his practice, but also those of a
number of his contemporaries who similarly chose to work with rational systems
in the interest of avoiding overt expressions of authorial subjectivity. See Sol
LeWitt, 'Paragraphs on Conceptual Art', *Artforum*, vol.5, no.10, Summer 1967,
pp.79—84; reprinted in Alexander Alberro and Blake Stimson (ed.), *Conceptual Art:
A Critical Anthology*, Cambridge, MA and London: The MIT Press, 1999, pp.12—16.
See also S. LeWitt, 'Sentences on Conceptual Art', *0—9*, no.5, July 1969, pp.3—5;
reprinted in A. Alberro and B. Stimson (ed.), *Conceptual Art: A Critical Anthology*,
op. cit., pp.106—08.

62
For this point, see Bernice Rose, 'Sol LeWitt and Drawing', in Alicia Legg (ed.),
Sol LeWitt (exh. cat.), New York: Museum of Modern Art, 1978, p.32.

63
S. LeWitt, 'Paragraphs on Conceptual Art', *Artforum, op. cit.*, p.80; or A. Alberro
and B. Stimson (ed.), *Conceptual Art: A Critical Anthology, op. cit.*, p.13.

64
Mel Bochner, 'Mel Bochner', *Data 2*, no.2, February 1972, p.64.

65
M. Bochner quoted in Yve-Alain Bois, 'The Measurement Pieces: From Index to
Implex', in Richard S. Field (ed.), *Mel Bochner: Thought Made Visible 1966—1973*
(exh. cat.), New Haven: Yale University Art Gallery, 1995, p.168.

66
Shown during the summer of 1970 (possibly June and/or July), Palermo's piece was
part of the inaugural program '14 × 14', organised by the recently appointed director

Klaus Gallwitz. The programme, spanning the years between 1968 and 1972,
gave young artists the opportunity to use the exhibition rooms of the Staatliche
Kunsthalle Baden-Baden for fourteen days to stage a sort of 'work in progress'
focusing on processual aspects in art and its relation to space. The seven double
exhibitions included Gerhard Richter, Günther Uecker, Georg Baselitz, Almut Heise,
Imi Knoebel, KRIWET, Markus Lüpertz, Ulrich Rückriem and Reiner Ruthenbeck,
amongst others.

67
Fred Sandback, 'Remarks on My Sculpture 1966—1986', in *Fred Sandback: Sculpture
1966—1986* (exh. cat.), Munich: Kunsthalle Mannheim, 1986, p.12.

68
Ibid., p.13.

69
For reasons of feasibility and to avoid damaging the gallery walls, new pipes were
ordered for the occasion.

70
Gordon Matta-Clark quoted in Florent Bex (ed.), *Gordon Matta-Clark* (exh. cat.),
Antwerp: International Cultureel Centrum, 1977, p.10.

71
Ibid.

72
Maria Nordman in conversation with the author, September 1997.

73
Ibid.

74
Ibid.

75
Marcel Broodthaers, 'Section des Figures', in Karl Ruhrberg and Jürgen Harten (ed.),
Der Adler vom Oligozän bis Heute (exh. cat.), Düsseldorf: Städtiche Kunsthalle, 1972,
vol.2, p.18. Translated by Angela Greiner for the author.

76
Some pieces were lent by the Sammlung Département des Aigles — in other words,
Broodthaers's private collection.

77
Every item in the exhibition possessed its own label with the statement 'This
is not a work of art' (taken from René Magritte) in French, German and English.
Explaining his strategy in the catalogue, Broodthaers proposed that his Duchampian
method of choosing non-art objects for museum exhibition was sustained by the
authority of the museum context as much as by his authorial prerogative to declare
— or, as in this case, deliberately attempt, albeit unsuccessfully, to disavow —

an object's status as art. See Marcel Broodthaers, 'Methode', in K. Ruhrberg and
J. Harten (ed.), *Der Adler vom Oligozän bis Heute, op. cit.*, vol.1, p.13.

78
In autumn 2005 the work was installed again, this time using red, a colour selected
by the curatorial staff as per the purchase conditions spelt out in the contract
with the artist, who proposed colours be chosen (and changed) over the years by
Art Institute curators.

79
The Santa Monica Museum of Art exhibition opened from 26 January to 12 April
2008; the Whitney exhibition was on view from 25 February to 30 May 2010.

80
For further discussion and documentation, see Miwon Kwon, 'Support and
Decoration: Michael Asher's Critique of the Architecture of Display', in Elsa
Longhauser (ed.), *Michael Asher* (exh. cat.), Santa Monica: Santa Monica Museum
of Art, 2008, unpaginated.

81
See Christopher Knight, 'Labyrinth from the Artist's Mind', *The Los Angeles Times*,
13 February 2008, http://articles.latimes.com/2008/feb/13/entertainment/
et-asher13 (last accessed on 3 April 2012).

82
Roberta Smith, 'How Art Is Framed: Exhibition Floor Plans as a Conceptual
Medium', *The New York Times*, 8 March 2008, http://www.nytimes.com/2008/03/08/
arts/08ashe.html (last accessed on 3 April 2012).

83
This was the case with, for example, 'The Peoples Choice (Arroz con Mango)', East
13th St, New York, 1981. The critical exhibition practice that Group Material
developed in the 1980s can be seen in part to be addressing questions that Asher's
work had began to open up in the 1970s.

84
See John Welchman (ed.), *Institutional Critique and After*, Zürich: JRP | Ringier,
2006; and A. Alberro and B. Stimson (ed.), *Institutional Critique: An Anthology of
Artists' Writings*, Cambridge, MA and London: The MIT Press, 2009.

85
See Judith E. Stein, 'Sins of Omission: Fred Wilson's *Mining the Museum*', *Art in
America*, no.81, October 1993, pp.110—15. See also Lisa G. Corrin (ed.), *Mining the
Museum: An Installation by Fred Wilson* (exh. cat.), New York: The New Press, 1994.

86
See A. Fraser, 'From the Critique of Institutions to an Institution of Critique',
Artforum, vol.44, no.1, September 2005, pp.278—83, 332; reprinted in A. Alberro
and B. Stimson (ed.), *Institutional Critique, op. cit.*, pp.408—17.

87
A. Alberro, 'Introduction: Mimicry, Excess, Critique', in A. Fraser, *Museum Highlights: The Writings of Andrea Fraser* (ed. A. Alberro), Cambridge, MA and London: The MIT Press, 2005, p.xxii.

88
See Barbara Pollack, 'Baring the Truth', *Art in America*, vol.90, no.7, July 2002, pp.86—87; A. Alberro, 'Introduction: Mimicry, Excess, Critique', *op. cit.*, pp.xxvi—xxvii; and A. Fraser, 'Museum Highlights: A Gallery Talk', in A. Fraser, *Museum Highlights*, *op. cit.*, pp.94—114, for the full script of this work as first published in *October*, vol.57, Summer 1991, pp.104—22.

89
See Andrea Fraser, 'Procedural Matters: On the Art of Michael Asher', *Artforum*, vol.46, no.10, Summer 2008, pp.375.

90
Maria Eichhorn, 'The Question of the Concept of Value', in A. Alberro and B. Stimson (ed.), *Institutional Critique*, *op. cit.*, p.389; and M. Eichhorn, *Maria Eichhorn: Das Geld der Kunsthalle Bern (Money at the Kunsthalle Bern)* (exh. cat.), vol.1 and 2, Bern: Kunsthalle Bern, 2001.

91
See Mai-Thu Perret, 'Maria Eichhorn', *frieze*, no.67, May 2002, p.92.